# The Power of Poems

## Writing Activities that Teach and Inspire

**Margriet Ruurs**

Second Edition

*The Power of Poems*
*Writing Activities that Teach and Inspire*
By Margriet Ruurs
Foreword by Arthur Black

Cover design:     Studio Montage
Book design:      Hank McAfee

**Library of Congress Cataloging-in-Publication Data**
Ruurs, Margriet.
  The power of poems : writing activities that teach and inspire / by Margriet Ruurs. -- Rev. 2nd ed.
       p. cm.
     Includes bibliographical references and index.
     ISBN 978-1-934338-89-6
    1. Poetry--Study and teaching (Elementary) 2. Poetry--Authorship--Study and teaching
(Elementary)--Activity programs. I. Title.
LB1575.R88 2011
372.64--dc22
                        2010047338

Maupin House publishes professional resources for K-12 educators. Contact us for tailored, in-school training or visit www.maupinhouse.com for free lesson plan downloads. Margriet Ruurs is available to speak at conferences and to visit schools, libraries, and art centers for author talks and professional development workshops throughout North America.

Other books by Margriet Ruurs:

| | | |
|---|---|---|
| *Virtual Maniac* | *My School in the Rainforest* | *My Librarian is a Camel* |
| *Amazing Animals* | *In My Backyard* | *Animal Alphabed* |
| *A Mountain Alphabet* | *I Live in the North* | *Ms. Bee's Magical Bookcase* |
| *Emma and the Coyote* | *Me & Martha Black* | *Wild Babies* |
| *Emma's Eggs* | *No Dogs Allowed* | *Emma's Cold Day* |
| *When We Go Camping* | *Wake Up, Henry Rooster!* | *Logan's Lake* |
| *Big Little Dog* | *Emma at the Fair* | *A Pacific Alphabet* |

Maupin House *by*
# capstone·
professional

Maupin House, Inc. by Capstone Professional
1710 Roe Crest Drive
North Mankato, MN 56003
1-800-524-0634, (fax) 352-373-5546
info@maupinhouse.com
www.maupinhouse.com

To Anne Wilson, Kate, and Sue
who gave me roots and wings as a writer.

## Acknowledgments

Special thanks to Sara Holbrook, Michael Salinger,
Avis Harley, David Booth, Ted Kooser, George Ella
Lyon, and Highlights for Children, Inc.,
as well as all the students who gave me
permission to use their poems.

And thanks to Kees, for putting up with me
while writing this book.

# Table of Contents

**Foreword**...................................................................................................................IX

**Introduction**.............................................................................................................XI

**Chapter 1: Poetry Philosophy**.........................................................................1

What is Poetry?...................................................................................................1

Why Poetry?.........................................................................................................2

How to Use This Book.......................................................................................3

How Do We Encourage the Writing of Poetry?.....................................5

Special Needs.....................................................................................................6

Time to Write......................................................................................................7

Oh, and One More Thing................................................................................7

Poetry and the Language Arts Standards.............................................9

Books to Support a Poetry-Rich Environment..................................10

Chapter 1: Bibliography and Websites...................................................12

**Chapter 2: Preparing for Poetry**................................................................13

Prerequisites of a Poetry Classroom......................................................13

Physical Environment............................................................................13

Freedom of Choice..................................................................................15

A Purpose to Write..................................................................................16

The Need for an Audience....................................................................17

Building Poetic Vocabulary.......................................................................18

Tools of the Trade...........................................................................................19

**Fitting Poetry into the Daily Schedule: Write Across the Curriculum** ... 22

    Social Studies ........................................................................... 23

    Math ........................................................................................ 24

    Science .................................................................................... 24

    Language Arts ......................................................................... 25

    Physical Education ................................................................... 25

    Music ...................................................................................... 25

    Art .......................................................................................... 26

    Other Times for Poetry ........................................................... 26

**Prewriting Activities** ...................................................................... 27

    Poems in a Box ........................................................................ 27

    Making a Picture File to Generate Ideas ................................ 28

    Making a Newspaper File to Generate Ideas ......................... 29

**A Few More Thoughts to Share . . .** ................................................ 32

**Chapter 2: Bibliography and Websites** .......................................... 33


**Chapter 3: Writing Activities** ........................................................ 36

**Prewriting Activity 1 — Wordstorming!** ....................................... 36

**Prewriting Activity 2 — Generating Ideas** .................................... 38

**Prewriting Activity 3 — Generating Ideas: "What If . . ."** .............. 40

**Writing Activity 1 — Inside Me** ..................................................... 41

**Writing Activity 2 — "What If . . ."** ................................................. 43

**Writing Activity 3 — Tongue Twisters and Nonsense** ................... 44

**Writing Activity 4 — Awesome Alliteration** .................................. 46

**Writing Activity 5 — Rhythm and Rhyme** ..................................... 48

**Writing Activity 6 — Painting Pictures with Words** ...................... 49

**Writing Activity 7 — Nature Poetry** .............................................. 54

**Writing Activity 8 — Music is Poetry** ............................................ 55

**Writing Activity 9 — And Poetry is Music!** .................................... 57

**Writing Activity 10 — Poems That Tell Stories** ............................. 58

**Writing Activity 11 — Metaphor and Simile** ................................. 60

    Metaphor ................................................................................ 60

    Simile ...................................................................................... 63

    "Guess What?" ........................................................................ 64

**Writing Activity 12 — Fortunately Poetry!** ................................... 65

**Writing Activity 13 — Poetry Workout** ......................................... 66

**Writing Activity 14 — Personal Favorites Poetry** ......................... 68

Writing Activity 15 — Times of Your Life ....................................... 69

Writing Activity 16 — Pick a Word, Any Word! ............................. 70

Writing Activity 17 — Picture Perfect Poems ............................... 72

Writing Activity 18 — Words That Paint Pictures ......................... 73

Writing Activity 19 — [Day] Dream Poems ................................... 74

Writing Activity 20 — S-e-n-s-ible Poems .................................... 76

    Poems You Can Smell! ................................................................. 76

    A Sound Poem ............................................................................. 76

    Feel That Poem! .......................................................................... 77

Writing Activity 21 — A Found Poem! ........................................... 81

Writing Activity 22 — Collecting Poems! ...................................... 83

Writing Activity 23 — Poetry Places ............................................. 84

Writing Activity 24 — Name Game ............................................... 91

Writing Activity 25 — Shape Poetry ............................................. 91

Writing Activity 26 — High-interest Poems .................................. 93

Writing Activity 27 — Memorizing a Poem ................................... 94

Writing Activity 28 — Seasonal Poetry ........................................ 96

Writing Activity 29 — Whose Viewpoint? ..................................... 98

Writing Activity 30 — Adding Rhyme to Reason ........................ 101

Writing Activity 31 — Take One Line and Add Words .................. 102

Writing Activity 32 — Personification ......................................... 103

Writing Activity 33 — Reflective Poetry ...................................... 105

Writing Activity 34 — Puzzle Poems ........................................... 108

Writing Activity 35 — Diamante Poems ...................................... 111

Writing Activity 36 — Shadow or Loop Poetry ............................ 113

Writing Activity 37 — Poems by Definition ................................. 116

Chapter 3: Bibliography and Websites ........................................ 119


**Chapter 4: The Editing Process** ................................................ 124

Critiquing .................................................................................... 124

Peer Conferencing ...................................................................... 126


**Chapter 5: Publishing and Sharing** ........................................... 130

The Need for an Audience .......................................................... 130

The Publishing Process .............................................................. 130

Designing and Illustrating Books ............................................... 131

    Typefaces ................................................................................. 132

Illustrations ............................................................... 133

Covers .................................................................... 134

About the Author ..................................................... 135

Assembling the Books ............................................... 136

Book Launch ................................................................ 137

Parents ................................................................... 137

Planning the Book Launch ........................................ 138

Invitations ............................................................... 138

Prep Time ............................................................... 138

More Ideas on Publishing in the Classroom ................... 140

Other Ways to Share and Celebrate ............................. 140

Submitting Poetry to Magazines .................................. 141

Magazines That Publish Writing by Children ............... 142

Publishing on the Internet ........................................... 143

Connecting with an Audience .................................. 145

Publishing an E-zine ............................................... 145

Chapter 5: Bibliography and Websites ......................... 148


After Words ................................................................... 151


Bibliography ................................................................. 154


Index ........................................................................... 164

*Publishing a volume of verse is like*
*dropping a rose petal down the*
*Grand Canyon and waiting for the echo.*

– Don Marquis

I can't remember exactly when I stopped reading poetry. Not in high school, for sure—I was mesmerized by Frost and Eliot, Pound and Dickinson. Not in my twenties either. Those years were saturated with the Beats and with Dylan. Not to mention a handsome, young Montreal man in a black leather jacket by the name of Cohen.

Actually, I never lost my love of poetry—it was contemporary poetry that did me in. Somewhere toward the hind end of the twentieth century, it seemed as if most poets turned their backs on the reading public in favor of playing increasingly obscure word games with each other. Poetry devolved into an exclusive ecosystem: poets writing coded messages for other poets, their editors, publishers, and close blood relations. Readers can take a hint; they left in droves. Nowadays in most bookstores, the Harry Potter shelf is longer than the entire poetry section. If there is a poetry section.

Which is a pity because poetry matters. Ideally, it is as good as writing gets. "Poetry is to prose," John Wain once said, "as dancing is to walking."

But things have changed since the days when a Frost or a Sandburg or a Robert Service could fill a concert hall for a reading. Today, a poetry comeback would have to compete not just with the conventional media, but also with the all-enveloping Internet—Facebook, YouTube, the entire Twitterverse.

But the battle isn't lost...yet. Poetry still works its magic on young ears, and poetry books for children still line the shelves of any self-respecting bookstore. That's where *The Power of Poems* comes in. This book not only opens young minds to the delights of poetry—traditional and contemporary—it also teaches them how to shape their own thoughts and perceptions poetically.

Margriet's love of poetry shines out from the pages of *The Power of Poems*. She's combined her ability to play with language with easy-to-use tools that you, the teacher, can use to pass on the magic of poetry to your students.

So read . . . enjoy . . . and pass on to the next generation.

*Arthur Black was the renowned host of Canada Broadcasting Corporation's national radio show,* Basic Black, *for nineteen years. He also wrote and hosted two award-winning TV shows and is the author a weekly humor column carried by more than fifty newspapers across Canada. He has fifteen books published to date and is a three-time winner of the Stephen Leacock Memorial Medal for Humour.*

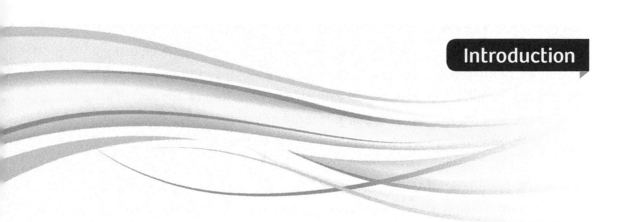

**po·et·ry,** *noun* \ˈpō-ə-trē, -i-trē *also* ˈpȯ(-)i-trē\ -

The Merriam-Webster dictionary defines poetry as "writing that formulates a concentrated imaginative awareness of experience in language chosen and arranged to create a specific emotional response through meaning, sound, and rhythm."

Look at how many words, in this one explanation alone, apply directly to all the important concepts we need to teach students: *imagination, awareness, language, emotional response.* The latter words, *meaning, sound,* and *rhythm*, are components that help make poetry an ideal format to teach these concepts in fun, attractive ways that can get students excited about and committed to writing their very own poems.

Throughout history, the greatest people have been inspired by poetry. Nelson Mandela was sustained by one poem (*Invictus* by William Hernest Henley) during twenty-seven dark years of cruel imprisonment. Mahatma Gandhi and Golda Meir were not writers, but they used poetry to inspire and to express their thoughts and feelings through sound and rhythm. Your students can do the same.

Since the first version of this book was published in 2001, I have had countless reactions from teachers across North America—indeed, from schools around the world—telling me how much they have enjoyed using the different writing exercises with their students. Many of them have sent me the results: a poem about the death of a grandfather, the loss of a dog, or the impact of 9/11. Whether it is large or small events, expressing feelings through poetry will help children cope with many emotions.

Some of these poems are now part of this revised book. It is my hope that more and more students will discover that they, too, can create a poem that touches someone else. From the specific comes the universal: if you write about your problem or joy, others will recognize it and take it to heart. Sharing poems allows you to recognize universal feelings, ideas, and concepts. Whether the poem is shared with one single person or published on the Internet, each and every poem written by a child has the potential to change his or her life. Twelve-year-old Hailey e-mailed me after her poem appeared in my online magazine, *Kidswwwrite* (**www. kalwriters.com/kidswwwrite**) and said: "I have always wanted to use my writing to change the world. Having my poems and stories published on your website has definitely boosted my 'writing self-confidence.'" "Writing self-confidence" is a skill that all kids can use. I believe it will help them get ahead in life, regardless of the direction they choose.

Poetry is not counting syllables or finding a rhyming word. It is playing with words—a celebration of language, regardless of what language you speak. I hope this book will inspire you to share the *joy* of reading and writing poetry with your students. As Winnie the Pooh says: "Poetry and hums aren't things which you get, they're things which get you. And all you can do is go where they can find you." (*Pooh's Little Instruction Book*, inspired by A. A. Milne.)

So come along, let's go there!

# Poetry Philosophy

Poetry is a wonderful resource for writing across the curriculum: lyrical language and rhythmic patterns provide opportunities for reading out loud, for memorization and choral speaking, as well as for independent reading and writing. Poetry can be incorporated into social studies and even sciences. Once children are hooked on the joy of reading and writing poetry, the skills will stay with them for a lifetime.

## What is Poetry?

As we saw earlier, the dictionary defines poetry as "a composition produced by creative imagination." How exciting it is to allow your students to use their creative imaginations to compose a piece of writing and help them learn at the same time! Because a poem is a story delivered in a rhythmical format, children who write poetry learn to express their creativity, develop and refine a variety of writing skills, and, in the process, have fun.

Poetry is a celebration of language, a play with words. It is music for the mind that can help a child tell a story in a unique way. Poetry is one of the earliest forms of literature to which children are exposed, and they love its natural rhythm and rhyme. Through nursery rhymes, lap games, and songs, children develop language. No wonder they like it: nursery rhymes, folktales, and ballads are some of the most pleasant, and earliest, forms of storytelling. These forms of poetry, through rich language, were used to teach morals and values as they entertained. Some nursery rhymes are, in fact, riddles. What a joy, not only to enjoy the sounds of the rhyme, but to discover the power in coming to understand the riddle and the secret message within.

Too many students have been exposed to a narrow range of poetry. Often, especially by the time they hit middle school, they feel that poetry has to be something serious. They do, however, fondly recall nursery rhymes or Dr. Seuss books.

Many students feel that poetry has to rhyme to be poetry. But it doesn't need to rhyme! Poetry can be whimsical. It can also be serious. Poetry is a form of writing usually written in shorter sentences than prose. The whole poem can be taken to heart and interpreted by each individual.

Poems can bring strong visual images to mind while speaking to the emotions. They help us to look at the world differently, to see something through different eyes. I read an anecdote in *Reader's Digest* in which a mother who never used makeup underwent a makeover. Her five-year-old looked at her face and exclaimed, "Mom! You look like a sunset!" That is poetry!

## Why Poetry?

Because poetry can be so satisfying and support a wide range of learning . . . Because the rhythm of poetry comes naturally to children . . . Because the potential of poetry lies within the minds of all children . . . . We need to nurture it with an abundance of words and then hand them the skills to refine and polish their writing.

Because the use of poetic language in the classroom brings along a certain energy, a joy that is hard to capture in prose . . . . Stories can be spellbinding, but poems have a special sort of magic that naturally appeals to kids and therefore makes it easy to introduce young students to reading and writing by means of poetry.

Writing your own poetry opens up the mind to a way of expressing oneself and allows the student to see the world through different eyes. A poem says something in a neat, unique package.

## How to Use This Book

In writing this book, it is my intent to help you teach the writing of poems to children. I soon realized, however, that we can't separate the writing from reading lots and lots of poems. So you will find, throughout this book, ways to start kids writing and reading poetry. I suggest you read the entire book first, for your own information, as well as to understand fully the structure of the activities.

The book addresses the following components of writing poetry:

**The content:** What are you writing about? Will your poem deal with an observation, a thought, a feeling, or perhaps tell a funny story? Will it have a message or simply be there to have fun with the words? Where do you get ideas?

**The craft:** How do you form the words into a poem? What tricks of the trade are there? How can you make use of sounds and rhythms to help shape your poem?

I don't think you can look at one component independently of the other; each builds on the other. You need to know what you want to write about, and learning more about the techniques of poetry helps you to do so more effectively. But what if you know all the techniques and have no idea what to write about? In this book, we will look at both aspects.

You can adapt this entire book easily to whichever grade level you teach by using different poetry books for younger or older students. I have aimed the activities at grades 3 to 8, but you can use them with your second graders or ninth graders just as well by adapting the books and poems you use as examples. The main bibliography at the end of this book is in alphabetical order by author, and I have also added a bibliography/list of additional resources at the end of each chapter. I hope that this makes it easier for you to quickly find a title.

The book will take you through the following steps:
- a look at how poetry will help your students and how it fits the curriculum;
- the prewriting process: tools you and your students need before the actual writing begins;
- generating ideas to create content: what to write about, where to get ideas;
- practical writing activities to learn the techniques, as well as expand the content;
- editing poems: learning the steps of refining the rough poem;
- publishing/sharing poems: the ultimate goal of writing a great poem!

I will begin by offering you suggestions for creating a poetry-friendly classroom, generating ideas, and beginning the prewriting process. The writing activities in Chapter 3 allow you to share different ways of creating poetry with your students. The activities are based on producing content, as well as on building technical skills. They are tried and true ways of writing that I have found to work well to get kids committed, and they are aimed at helping you discover the enjoyment and excitement of using poetry in the classroom on a daily basis. The order in which the writing activities are presented allows students' writing skills to grow and expand throughout the process.

I recommend that you use Prewriting Activities 1-3 and Writing Activities 4 and 5 in that order. The activities that follow these foundations can be used whenever they suit your schedule. Chapter 4 will help you and your students to critique and edit the poems. Chapter 5 has suggestions for publishing and sharing your students' poetry, both in print and on the Internet.

## How Do We Encourage the Writing of Poetry?

As teachers, we have an obligation to let children experience the joy of reading and writing poetry. To do that successfully, the child has to be motivated to write. To truly motivate a child to be a writer, we need to do more than teach specific skills. When I was a child, I used to hate having to analyze poetry. I didn't want to explain why I liked a particular sentence or guess at what the author meant when he or she wrote that line. I just wanted to enjoy the poem for what it was. I wanted to savor the sounds, the rhythm, and maybe try writing my own poems.

There is much more to teaching poetry to children than teaching specific skills or having them "dissect" poems. When students visit a museum, they're not allowed to scratch at the varnish of a painting or turn the canvas over to see what's underneath: they observe and absorb the complete piece as a work of art, taking it to mind as a whole.

Let's treat poetry the same way. Let's enjoy and savor the words. It's okay not to like a certain poem or to love another one. We can't all like the same thing. But let's submerge our kids in poetic language. Once they have built up a vocabulary and have mastered some of the poetry-writing techniques, then we can take a closer look at different structures of poems and delve deeper into meaning and style.

As a writer, I don't believe that writers write poetry to have a reader guess at what they might have meant. A writer creates with imagination so that a reader can make the poem his or hers and savor it for what it means to him or her. Teachers must be careful not to impose on students their own views of what a poem means. Let the children take the poem to heart and interpret it for themselves. Sometimes poems are pieces of writing just to be savored.

When first embarking upon a poetry course, students sometimes confess that they don't really like poetry. What a great challenge to prove to them that poetry need not be boring! Let's take that challenge and find ways of writing poetry that appeal to students and allow them to play with words! The learning will follow.

Remember how nice it felt to squeeze Play-Doh between your fingers and make whatever shapes came to mind? Maybe we should treat language like Play-Doh when we write poetry. When we use our imagination and play with words, it's exciting to see the shape of the poem that emerges.

## Special Needs

Although all students can benefit from poetry, it is an especially useful genre to use with those who are learning English as a second language. Introducing poetry to these students will help them learn through rhythm, sounds, and repetition. No matter what the age of the student, poetry can help familiarize him or her with the sounds of our language. Many advanced picture books are written in rhyme and are suitable for middle and high school students, for example:

- *Animalia* by Graeme Base
- *Aska's Animals* by Warabé Aska and David Day
- *There Were Monkeys in My Kitchen* by Sheree Fitch

For younger ESL kids, simple nursery rhymes and games will help ease the tension of learning a new language, for example:

- *Bear in Mind: A Book of Bear Poems* by Bobbye S. Goldstein
- *The Candlewick Book of First Rhymes* by Candlewick Press
- *Edward the Emu* by Sheena Knowles
- *More Surprises* (an "I Can Read Book") by Lee Bennett Hopkins

Students with learning disabilities can often produce poetry with a tape recorder or word processor. Dictation works wonderfully with those students who haven't quite mastered writing skills and who become impatient when they can't write down their thoughts fast enough.

I once worked with a severely physically and mentally disabled student. She wrote poetry and sent it to me via e-mail. I read and critiqued her poems, and she responded by editing and rewriting. Her love for language showed itself in her writing. I had no idea that she was disabled until her teacher told me. The use of a computer allowed her to participate in writing to her full capacity. Her teacher added that she had never been so committed or so enthusiastic about anything. Poetry allowed her thoughts to take flight.

## Time to Write

Once you embark on your journey of poetry, you will need to make time for it. If you have never taught poetry in your classroom, start by reading a poem a day. Use one in language arts; the next day, use one during math. Slowly increase the number of poems you use. Once you are ready to have students write their own poetry, set aside at least half an hour a day. When your students really get into the writing, and when you plan to classroom-publish books of poetry (see Chapter 5), allow at least an hour a day.

## Oh, and One More Thing . . .

While looking at all the ways in which to write and to introduce poetry to kids, let's not forget to simply have fun with the process! You may notice that, in this book about poetry, I won't dwell on the forms of haiku or limerick. The reason is simple: I don't like having to count syllables while being creative. Another rule I have while writing poetry is not to think too much. Just write, have fun with words, and enjoy what you are creating! I have seen this rule to be very liberating for students. Try it in your classroom!

While engaged in meaningful writing, children need to enjoy the process if we hope to turn them into lifelong writers. If it isn't fun, how can you get excited about it? Having fun picking a subject, having fun writing, and having fun sharing and reading out loud will make everything else easier. After all, when you're having fun, writing poetry will simply be a breeze!

Making up stories and playing with language can be just that—pure fun. Most writers write because it is what they love to do most. Heaven knows they don't do it for the pay!

However, writing for fun is not frivolous: it plays a role in the long-term development of the craft of writing itself. When it's fun, you'll want to keep practicing it. Within the fun are power and purpose.

The joy of writing poetry can be contagious if it is an engaging and rewarding experience. Writing is an important part of real learning. The use of "real language" implies an authentic meaning: language used by real people for a variety of real purposes and real consequences. When we share our love of reading and writing with children, we should, therefore, use real language and real books—as opposed to basal readers. We should also let them write authentic stories. Using drill sheets or fill-in-the-blank types of activities may help to teach a child the rules of sentence structure or grammar but cannot, and never will, get that child excited about writing.

After discussing how to teach your students to write poems, we will look at how your students can share their poetry—because, without a real audience to address, what's the use of writing? If I didn't hope that you would be reading this someday, why would I bother putting all this down on paper? I write in hopes of sharing ideas and suggestions with you, in hopes of working together so that we may stimulate children to discover the joy that writing can bring.

Joy doesn't come from filling in the blanks. Joy comes from someone's response to your writing, from seeing someone else laugh or cry when they read your words. Wow! That's powerful stuff. So, are you ready? Let's picture a student who challenges us by saying, "Make me *want* to write poems," and let's do just that!

## Poetry and the Language Arts Standards

The activities in this book pertain directly to the skills targeted by state and provincial language arts standards for grades 3 through 8. Please check your own state or provincial requirements to see how each activity meets specific standards.

U.S. national language arts standards expect students to learn to think critically, solve problems, communicate clearly, and be able to learn and work both independently and with others. Students are expected to employ a wide range of strategies as they write and to use different writing-process elements appropriately to communicate with disparate audiences for a variety of purposes. The writing activities in this book contribute to this outcome by providing a framework to help students:

- develop reading and writing skills;
- present and respond to ideas, feelings, and knowledge sensitively and creatively;
- use poetry as a way of developing personal values, understanding multicultural heritage, and broadening experience;
- use language confidently to understand and respond thoughtfully to factual and imaginative communications in speech, print, and the media;
- express themselves powerfully and gracefully for a variety of personal and social purposes;
- use language appropriate to the audience and purpose;
- become comfortable with the format of poetry.

For some of the English K-12 national standards (United States) that are met by the activities in this book, see the NCTE/IRA Standards for Language Arts: **http://www.ncte.org/standards**.

Canada does not have national standards. However, each province has its own guidelines and targets. For examples of standards from British Columbia that are met through the activities in this book, visit the Ministry of Education section of the Government of British Columbia website (**http://www.bced.gov.bc.ca/irp/welcome.php**)and select "English Language Arts" under the "by Subject" drop-down menu.

Whether you have already taught or written much poetry or whether you have not yet tackled it, this book will support you in letting poetry flow throughout your curriculum for the sheer pleasure of sharing. By showing you how to throw a poetry party during socials, use poetry to inspire your art curriculum, include the lyrics of a song during music lessons, and add some rhythm to math, I will help you to do so.
Then, poetry will truly come alive in your classroom!

## Books to Support a Poetry-Rich Environment

These titles will support you in selecting the best titles and techniques to use poetry in your classroom:

Booth, David. *Classroom Voices.* Toronto: Harcourt Brace, 1994.

Booth, David. *Literacy Techniques: For Building Successful Readers and Writers.* Markham, Ont.: Pembroke Publishers, 1996.

Booth, David, and Bill Moore. *Poems Please! Sharing Poetry with Children.* Markham, Ont. Pembroke Publishers, 1988.

Brownlie, Faye, Susan Close, and Linda Wingren. *Reaching for Higher Thought: Reading, Writing, Thinking Strategies.* Edmonton, Alberta: Arnold Publishing, 1988.

Brownlie, Faye, Susan Close, and Linda Wingren. *Tomorrow's Classroom Today: Strategies for Creating Active Readers, Writers, and Thinkers.* Portsmouth, N.H.: Heinemann, 1990.

Buzzeo, Toni, and Jane Kurtz. *Terrific Connections with Authors, Illustrators and Storytellers: Real Space and Virtual Links.* Westport, Conn.: Libraries Unlimited, 1999.

Calkins, Lucy McCormick. *Lessons from a Child: On the Teaching and Learning of Writing.* Portsmouth, N.H.: Heinemann, 1983.

Crossley-Holland, Kevin. *Once Upon a Poem.* Frome, Somerset: Chicken House Publishing, 2004.

Esbensen, Barbara Juster. *A Celebration of Bees: Helping Children Write Poetry.* New York: Henry Holt, 1995.

Fox, Mem. *Radical Reflections: Passionate Opinions on Teaching, Learning, and Living.* New York: Mariner Books, 1993.

Freeman, Marcia S. *Building a Writing Community: A Practical Guide.* Gainesville, FL: Maupin House Publishing, 1997.

Goforth, Frances S. *Literature & the Learner.* New York: Wadsworth Publishing Company, 1998.

Hopkins, Lee Bennett. Pass the Poetry, Please!. New York, HarperCollins, 1998. Jobe, Ron, and Mary Dayton-Sakari. *Reluctant Readers: Connecting Students and Books for Successful Reading Experiences.* Markham, Ont.: Pembroke Publishers, 1999.

Jobe, Ron, and Paula Hart. *Canadian Connections: Experiencing Literature with Children.* Markham, Ont.: Pembroke Publishers, 1991.

Knowles, Sheena. *Edward the Emu*, HarperCollins, 1998

Little, Jean. *I Gave My Mom a Castle.* Custer, Wash.: Orca Book Publishers, 2003.

Moore, William H., *Words That Taste Good: More than 600 Short, Sharp, Sparkling Bits of Poetry.* Markham, Ont.: Pembroke Publishers, 1987.

Nodelman, Perry. *The Pleasures of Children's Literature.* New York: Longman Publishing Group, 1992.

Spink, John. *Children as Readers: A Study.* London: Clive Bingley, 1989.

# Chapter 1: Bibliography and Websites

## BIBLIOGRAPHY

*The Candlewick Book of First Rhymes.* Cambridge, Mass.: Candlewick Press, 1996.

Base, Graeme. *Animalia*, New York: Harry N. Abrams, 1986.

Crossley-Holland, Kevin. *Once Upon a Poem.* Frome, Somerset: Chicken House Publishing, 2004.

Day, David, and Warabé Aska. *Aska's Animals.* Toronto: Doubleday Canada, 1991.

Fitch, Sheree. *There Were Monkeys in My Kitchen.* Toronto: Doubleday Canada, 1992.

Goldstein, Bobbye S. *Bear in Mind: A Book of Bear Poems.* New York: Viking Kestrel, 1989.

Hopkins, Lee Bennett. *More Surprises* (an "I Can Read Book"). New York: Harper & Row, 1987.

## WEBSITES

To view an Integrated Resource Package providing information about English Language Arts (K-7) for teachers in British Columbia, Canada, visit the British Columbia Ministry of Education website: **www.bced.gov.bc.ca/ irp/irp.htm.**

To view a list of provincial expectations for all language arts programs (K-8) in Ontario, Canada, visit the Ontario Ministry of Education website: **http:// www.edu.gov.on.ca/eng/curriculum/elementary/language18currb.txt.**

*The Standards for the English Language Arts* is required reading for English language arts professionals at all levels as it complements national, state, and local standards and discusses curricula and classroom activities. To view the document, visit the NCTE website: **http://www.ncte.org/standards**.

# Preparing for Poetry

## Prerequisites of a Poetry Classroom

In this chapter, we will go over the prewriting process: tools you and your students need before the actual writing begins.

### PHYSICAL ENVIRONMENT

A physical environment conducive to writing poetry is a classroom that is saturated with words. Books, a reading corner, poems on the wall, and scrap paper to use when an idea "hits" should all be readily available.

The more you read, the better a writer you'll be. Therefore, I recommend that you supply a wide variety of poetry for students to read and look through. In *Literature and the Learner*, Frances S. Goforth says: "Saturate children with a variety of poems representing various poetic forms, types, and elements."

Here is a sample selection of books of poetry particularly suited to be read out loud. Display as many as you can find of these and other favorite titles:

- *Alligator Pie* by Dennis Lee
- *Barn Dance!* by Bill Martin Jr. and John Archambault

- *Dinosaurs,* selected by Lee Bennett Hopkins
- *Falling Up* by Shel Silverstein
- *I Can Read with My Eyes Shut!* by Dr. Seuss
- *A Lucky Thing* by Alice Schertle
- *Poetry Party* by Bruce Lansky
- *Rainbows, Head Lice, and Pea-Green Tile: Poems in the Voice of the Classroom Teacher* by Brod Bagert
- *Scared Silly! A Book for the Brave* by Marc Brown
- *Something Big Has Been Here* by Jack Prelutsky
- *Toes in My Nose: And Other Poems* by Sheree Fitch
- *What's on the Menu?* selected by Bobbye S. Goldstein

Reading aloud from books of poetry will help students extend their vocabulary while hearing the structure of sentences, the meter of the poem, and the use of techniques, such as metaphor or alliteration.

See the bibliography at the end of this chapter for more books particularly suited for reading out loud.

Even, or perhaps I should say, particularly, if you teach upper middle school, supply your students with Shakespeare, as well as with Dr. Seuss, Bill Pete, and Roald Dahl. I was once asked to address the graduating class of our high school. Rather than composing a boring speech, I chose to read them *Oh, the Places You'll Go!* by Dr. Seuss. His eloquent words evoked both laughter and tears. No one could have summed up the sentiments for such an occasion better. Years later, at a supermarket checkout, the clerk told me she was in that graduating class and how much they all had loved hearing that poem!

The physical environment also should offer students a comfortable writing space. That can be at their desks, but it may also be on the floor or in a corner. Before allowing my students this choice, I have made the rule clear: "You can sit anywhere you like as long as you write hard." They know that if they don't concentrate on their writing, they lose the privilege of choosing a workspace. If you decide to allow students to write where they find themselves most comfortable, be sure to hold them responsible for their behavior. One teacher I know purchased large, cedar-chip filled dog pillows and has them available as comfortable reading/ writing spots. Keep on hand a supply of scrap paper, lined paper, and pencils for when that great idea strikes.

As I mentioned in the previous chapter, allow sufficient time in your daily schedule to write. Increase the amount of time as your students become more skilled. They will start to ask for more time as their enjoyment of the writing increases.

A book that is not a book of poetry but is still one you might want to include in your display is *Oh, the Places He Went* by Maryann N. Weidt. This biography of Dr. Seuss will interest anyone who likes his writing. Books of poetry, as well as books about poets, are valuable resources to inspire new writers.

Another delicious book about poetry to read aloud is *The Bat-Poet* by Randall Jarrell.

## FREEDOM OF CHOICE

Let's look at some necessary ingredients for successful poetry writing. Choice of topic is important in motivating kids to read, as well as to write. When you go to the library, you have a wealth of choices available. No one tells you which book you must read. You choose according to your own personal tastes and interests. Perhaps you pick a specific genre or a topic about which you want to learn more. Perhaps you choose your favorite author. But the choice is yours.

Exposing students to a wide variety of topics, genres, and authors gives them an opportunity to develop their own preferences. Even if the choice is limited to the number of books in your classroom, the student makes his or her own choice and will be more committed to reading the book than if it were assigned without options.

The same holds true for writing. When kids are free to choose their own topics, even if given a limited range of topics from which to choose, they will be more committed to the writing process. If you told me to write about, say, dinosaurs, I would have a hard time committing because I'm not particularly interested in dinosaurs. But, if you gave me a choice of animals, I might research and write about . . . ladybugs! I might just be in to ladybugs right now.

I could find out why they are called ladybugs, what purpose they serve in nature, or even write a ladybug poem! Next month, I might want to write about blizzards or mountain climbing – or, while the World Cup is in the news, I might want to write a soccer poem!

Parents have sometimes asked me if they should be concerned because their child was only interested in one particular topic and wouldn't write about anything else—poems about racecars, stories about racecars, nonfiction about racecars. I believe we should applaud that kind of intense interest. Feed that interest by giving your students more resources on the topic, more books to read. Let them read, let them research, let them write. Jim's interest in racecars may not interest you and it may even last for a whole year, but eventually he'll move on to something else. In the process, he'll acquire crucial skills for reading, researching, and writing.

By grades 8 or 9, many kids are intrigued by the topic of death. I have seen happy, well-balanced kids write very serious poems about death or suicide. Writing might just be the healthy way to deal with such complex issues at that age. Their pieces of writing may even lead to wonderful discussions of the topic, giving you an opportunity to allay fears and to be in tune with your students' concerns.

## A PURPOSE TO WRITE

All authors write for a real purpose, so why shouldn't children? If your students have no idea what the purpose of a writing assignment is, or if their only purpose is to get a mark, they won't put their heart and soul into it. In these cases, their writing won't reflect true feelings nor will it have the quality that it would have if the students have a more meaningful purpose and truly care about their writing.

Often, the purpose of writing a poem will be self-expression. The purpose of creating tongue twisters or silly rhymes can be purely to have fun with language. And, at some point, the purpose of writing another poem will be to complete a book. But mostly, we will look at poems as a way to put thoughts and feelings into a package that is fun to create and that appeals to the reader.

Of course, the more you write, the more skilled you become. Writing for practice may be one reason to write; so, if we can package the practice into fun, engaging activities, it will also serve a real purpose for students. When students have a true purpose to write, they show more commitment and the enthusiasm to write more.

## THE NEED FOR AN AUDIENCE

All authors write so that someone will read their writing. Students can find meaning in writing by realizing who their audiences are. As teachers or parents, we can demonstrate the joy of reading as we share a genuine interest in the contents of a poem.

By reading out loud a text that has captivated us, made us cry, or made us laugh, we can show children the true reason for reading and writing. If children realize why we read, they will be more motivated to learn how to read—as well as how to write. Thirteen-year-old Stephanie was frightened and confused after watching the devastation of 9/11 on television. Her father gave her pencil and paper. Stephanie wrote the following poem to deal with her feelings.

## Harbor View

*I stand here in the harbor,*
*my torch held up high.*
*I could not stop the planes*
*that came and passed me by.*
*My children are in danger*
*as I watch them run and hide.*
*The Towers soon collapse,*
*while some are trapped inside.*
*I try to shout out warnings,*
*but do not have that choice.*
*Although my name is Liberty,*
*I was built without a voice.*

The power of a poem such as this one comes not from finding words that rhyme, but from looking for a way to express thoughts and feeling. Realizing whom we write for (peers, younger children, adults, etc.) will help the writing. I write very differently when composing a letter to an old friend than when I write a formal thank-you note. An article about teaching is aimed at a different audience than a short story for a children's magazine. Knowing my audience influences my style of writing. Of course, the author may also write just for him or herself. Sharing writing with an audience is something we will look at in greater detail in Chapter 5.

## Building Poetic Vocabulary

To write poems, kids need access to a wide variety of words. The more words are available, the greater the fun of finding just the right one to go into your sentence. Prepare your students for writing poetry by "wordstorming." Prewriting Activity 1 in Chapter 3 deals with wordstorming. It will guide you to select a topic and generate words on that topic, giving your students access to lots of good sounds. Once they get used to the concept of wordstorming, students can suggest their own topics.

Wordstorm often. This activity will increase your students' vocabulary and open their eyes to the possibilities of a poem.

When you make lists of words and ideas on the board, keep a copy on paper for future reference. You could instruct all students to write down the words as you wordstorm, or one student could be assigned to be the scribe.

## Tools of the Trade

At first, language is the only tool children need to write poems: lots of words to describe their thoughts and feelings—words that enable them to see something in a new light. Poetic language comes naturally to children, and many will already be using concepts of which they do not know the technical terms or definitions.

Dr. Seuss once said that "writing with shorth is harder than writing with length." Poems use "shorth," and by choosing just the perfect word, you can paint a picture of the image you are trying to convey. In a poem, you don't have room to explain or to describe in detail. So finding just the right word is even more important than in other genres.

As their poetic vocabulary grows, students can create a wider variety of poems. Learning about the craft options available helps kids grow as poets.

I don't believe that we should throw these writing terms at them until they have "tasted" the joy of writing poems from the heart. I mention the terms here for you, the teacher, but the writing activities for students that focus on these technical skills will come later (Writing Activity 4 and higher). Once students have been introduced to the basics of poetry writing and you know that they are ready to learn more, then gently present them with more techniques. For definitions, I have referred to the *Harbrace College Handbook* by John C. Hodges and Mary E. Whitten (HBJ Canada, 1986).

**Alliteration** is the repetition of the same sound. It can include both consonants and vowels (Emma's eggs; a great grizzly). Alliteration is one of the earliest techniques of poetry. This is another strong tool in crafting poetry, but we sometimes need to caution emerging writers not to overuse it!

**Metaphor** is a figure of speech that compares two dissimilar things, for example, snowflakes to cotton balls or the ocean to a dragon. Metaphor is a strong tool to use in writing poetry and one that kids often already use unconsciously.

**Onomatopoeia** refers to a word that imitates the sound the object makes: *moo, hiss, cuckoo.* This technique has often been used in nursery rhymes.

**Personification** attributes human characteristics to non-human things, such as animals or objects. (The flowers danced in the field; a grouchy ladybug). A great tool to use when writing poetry, personification allows a tree to talk or a cloud to think!

**Simile** is also a comparison but using the words *like* or *as.* ("The sky is as black *as* ink." "Your face looks *like* the sunset.")

**Rhythm** is the beat or meter of a word or sentence. Rhythm is determined by the number of syllables and spaces in a line and can be used to obtain a certain effect in your poem. You can best hear the rhythm of a poem by reading it aloud. Poets can use short words to make short-sounding sentences or choose long words that fall into a certain rhythm.

**Rhyme** is created by using similar sounding words at the end of a sentence (cat—fat; dirty—thirty; bicycle—icicle). I hope you noticed that I didn't mention rhyme until now. All kids can rhyme, but writing a rhyming poem can be very restricting. Often, kids think that in order for it to be a real poem, it has to rhyme. On the contrary, if the rhyme makes the story line stilted, don't rhyme!

This is the first of three common rhyme schemes:

A    A    B    B

Here, the first and second lines rhyme, and the third and fourth lines
rhyme, as in:

> A girl named Anna-Belle-Lou
> said, "I don't like my hair blonde, I want it blue!"
> She painted her hair, not orange or green
> but the bluest blue that you've ever seen!

> ("Anna-Belle-Lou" from *Virtual Maniac*)

Another rhyme scheme is:

A    B    A    B

Here, the first sentence rhymes with the third and the second sentence
rhymes with the fourth, as in:

> I like making music with my voice
> with notes in high and low.
> It's such a joyful, cheerful noise
> I wonder why my brother hates it so?!

> ("Singing" from *Virtual Maniac*)

Another rhyme scheme is:

A   B   B   A

Here, the first and last sentence of a stanza rhyme, and the second and third lines rhyme, as in:

> Like a bird in the sky
> I soar down the slope.
> Faster and faster, I hope
> I get wings and can fly!

("Downhill" from Virtual Maniac)

To stay with this line of thinking—to speak in a metaphor—I will compare writing poetry to carpentry. Give kids a piece of wood, and they will turn it into whatever their imagination tells them it is. By the time others can recognize its shape, it is still rough.

We need to take a piece of sandpaper to smooth the shape, to get rid of the splinters, and to make it something that will be kept and treasured. Sometimes a poem will come out perfectly without needing any sanding. At other times, applying some of the above-mentioned techniques to the rough shape will turn the piece of poetry into a treasure.

## Fitting Poetry into the Daily Schedule: Write Across the Curriculum

Besides spending time to work specifically on poetry, try to sneak poems into other daily activities. Poetry fits easily into your daily schedule if you use the format to inform, to read, and to write. You can incorporate poetry that informs as well as excites into different areas of your curriculum. Let's take a look at the way poetry can fit into specific content areas:

## SOCIAL STUDIES

Poetry has strong oral roots. Poetry is found throughout history around the world. Ballads were popular ways of telling stories in the Middle Ages. Many native people use poetry to narrate stories and legends. Use texts that give information about a period, an event, or places.

When studying the Middle Ages, read *Good Masters! Sweet Ladies! Voices from a Medieval Village* by Laura Amy Schlitz.

When studying World Wars, use Linda Granfield's books:

- *High Flight: A Story of World War II*
- *In Flanders Fields: The Story of the Poem by John McCrae*
- *Remembering John McCrae: Soldier - Doctor - Poet*

When studying the North, incorporate:

- "The Cremation of Sam McGee" by Robert Service
- *Polar Bear, Arctic Hare: Poems of the Frozen North* by Eileen Spinelli
- "The Spell of the Yukon" by Robert Service, from *The Best of Robert Service*

To learn place names, use:

- "A Wonderful Trip in a Rocketship" by Dennis Lee, from *The Ice Cream Store*
- "Kleena Kleene" by Margriet Ruurs, from *Virtual Maniac*
- *Got Geography!* by Lee Bennett Hopkins

## MATH

Why not lighten up a math problem by reading a math poem?

When you demonstrate to students how a poem can be used, even during the math period, it sends a strong message about the importance of reading and literacy. These poems, and others, can lighten the mood when tackling difficult subject but can also encourage a student to try again:

- "Countdown" by Jack Prelutsky, from *Scared Silly*
- "Five Fat Fleas" by Dennis Lee, from *Jelly Belly*
- *There Was An Old Woman* by Steven Kellogg (Try counting and subtracting the things she eats in this zany book!)
- *Math-terpieces* by Greg Tang
- *The Grapes of Math* by Greg Tang
- *Math Poetry, Linking Language & Math in a Fresh Way* by Betsy Franco

## SCIENCE

Demonstrate how the subject of science has been used by writers. Read some of the following titles during science lessons, not only to support your science curriculum through literacy, but to show students a fresh angle on certain topics:

- *Science Verse* by Jon Scieszka and Lane Smith
- *Scien-Trickery: Riddles in Science* by Frank Remkiewicz
- *Spectacular Science: A Book of Poems* by Lee Bennett Hopkins

When studying the environment, use poetry to discuss topics such as environmental awareness, water pollution and preservation by reading books like:

- *The Sign of the Seahorse* by Graeme Base
- *The Water Hole* by Graeme Base

## LANGUAGE ARTS

The writing of poetry, of course, fits certain requirements of your language arts curriculum. But books of poetry also can add to the general learning of words, sentence structure, the alphabet, and more–not just when you teach poetry. Here are some poems and books that you can display in your classroom to use when teaching language arts:

- *Aster Aardvark's Alphabet Adventures* by Steven Kellogg (alliteration)
- "The Alphabet from Z to A" by Judith Viorst, from *The Alphabet from Z to A (With Much Confusion on the Way)* (alliteration)
- *The Eleventh Hour* by Graeme Base (a book full of riddles, missing letters, and puzzles in which kids have to solve a mystery)
- "My Snake" by Jack Prelutsky, from *Something Big Has Been Here* (This poem is about a snake that can make the entire alphabet, and it is hilarious. It can be used to perform, as well!)
- *I Know an Old Laddie* by Jean Little (Variation on the well known "I Know An Old Woman," this poem is full of wonderful rhythm and word play)
- *If I Had a Paka* by Charlotte Pomerantz (a book of poems in eleven languages! You learn Swahili, Dutch, Croatian, and even Native American words through the well-crafted poems)

## PHYSICAL EDUCATION

There are even poems to use before or after P.E. class:

- *Extra Innings: Baseball Poems* by Lee Bennett Hopkins
- *Hoops* by Robert Burleigh
- *Red Dog, Blue Fly: Football Poems* by Sharon Bell Mathis
- "Transformation" by Gordon Korman, from *The Last Place Sports Poems of Jeremy Bloom*

## MUSIC

Writing Activities 8 and 9 focus on poetry as music. These activities are easily adaptable to suit your own music curriculum. In addition, you can have students perform or recite poetry from memory while accompanying them on instruments. Have students match instruments to the tone of the poem: gentle bells and triangles for spring rain, a repetitive boom on the tambourine for a giant's footsteps, and so on.

A wonderful book to use with grades 4 and up is *The Worst Band in the Universe* by Graeme Base. This wild poetic tale deals with musicians and instruments and is accompanied by a CD-ROM. The book *Amazing Grace: The Story of the Hymn* by Linda Granfield can also be studied to see how some poetry becomes music that lasts throughout the ages.

## ART

Many picture books, often in poetry, can be used by art teachers, not just because of their glorious illustrations, which can be used as inspiration for students' own art, but also because their subjects make them suitable for use in art class:

- *Images of Nature: Canadian Poets and the Group of Seven* selected by David Booth
- *Two by Two* by Barbara Reid (illustrated in Plasticine)
- *In My Backyard* by Margriet Ruurs (illustrated by Ron Broda in paper sculptures)
- *Window* by Jeannie Baker (collage)
- *Listen to the Wind* by Greg Mortensen (illustrated with scraps of fabric)
- *Zoom* by Istvan Banyai (which, like a camera, zooms out from an object)

## OTHER TIMES FOR POETRY

When assigning homework, have fun by reading a homework poem like one of these:

- "Certainly I Did My Homework" by Gordon Korman, from *The D-Poems of Jeremy Bloom*
- "My Dog Chewed Up My Homework" by Bruce Lansk, from *Poetry Party*

If your school is undergoing accreditation, read *Hooray for Diffendoofer Day!* by Dr. Seuss and Jack Prelutsky. Not only will your students love it, but it will lift the mood of staff and parents as well.

There are food poems and boot poems, rainy poems and sunny poems, bedtime poems, and principal poems. There are poems about bats and frogs and, probably more than any other topic, books of poetry about dinosaurs! You can read a loud poem out loud or tape a quiet poem to the door without saying anything. Use enriching poems throughout your day, not just during language arts.

## Prewriting Activities

Before the actual *writing* process, introduce students to poetry by reading it. Share poems from books, read one aloud, read a joke poem, or share a beautiful poem about feelings. Read a dinosaur poem or a rainbow poem just to show how much fun is packed into the format of a poem.

### POEMS IN A BOX

To promote the daily use of poems, start a Poetry Box. Use a cardboard box decorated with words and pictures labeled "Poems Please" to stimulate the reading and writing of poems. Give the box a prominent place in the classroom and tell the students that you will put some of your favorite poems in it. Each day, you will pull out a poem to read. Invite students to contribute their favorite poems. They can copy a poem from a book or magazine or write their own. You could suggest literary websites as other sources for finding poems to share (be sure to include credit to the author when you read someone else's poem).

Each day, as you read a poem from the box, students will show more interest. At first, you might be the one who reads the daily poem, but soon your students will be eager to do the reading. Within a short period of time, you may be reading several poems a day. As they gain confidence as writers, the children will contribute more self-written poems. This activity not only encourages students to write, but it also makes them read, and listen to, more poems.

## MAKING A PICTURE FILE TO GENERATE IDEAS

Start looking for funny or interesting pictures in magazines, cut them out, and keep them in a box or file folder. This file will form a foundation for storytelling and poetry writing activities. Look specifically for pictures that seem to have a story behind them. What is happening in the picture? What just happened? What will happen next? Who is the main character? Who else is or might be there? What's the story?

Pictures that I have collected include images from:

- ads for pet food:
    - a cat in an Oriental vase
    - a cat licking its lips in a pantry full of food
    - a dog with a bandana, looking very pooped
- ads for carpet cleaners:
    - gigantic, upside-down ice-cream cone on a floor
    - little bugs that look like tiny aliens
- ads for floor wax:
    - a family and an elephant at the breakfast table
    - boy tracking mud all over the house

I have found pictures of dancing carrots, of a beaver lodge with a chimney and a porch, of a girl riding on a polar bear's back, of two men sailing in a shoe.

When you start to look for pictures, you'll discover that many advertisements are very suitable as storytelling pictures. It might take you a little while to find good ones, but I'm sure you'll build a great collection. Keep looking and eventually replace the iffy pictures in your collection with ones that are more apt.

Another great place to find good illustrations to generate story ideas is publishers' catalogues. Most book publishers issue a catalogue of new books once or twice a year. These show book illustrations for new books, as well as books on their backlist. Cut out the illustrations and glue them on a sheet of construction paper.

Laminate your picture collection to ensure a longer life. Store them in a manila file folder or large envelope. I will refer to this picture file in Writing Activity 17.

## MAKING A NEWSPAPER FILE TO GENERATE IDEAS

It is often said that truth is more amazing than fiction. Newspaper articles provide some of the best sources for ideas, as newspapers are full of amazing happenings. We can use these stories as starting points for creating our own amazing poems. Students can use fictional names, fictional settings, and add as much to the story as they like.

Start looking for and selecting sample stories. These can simply be stories that you like and that you feel you could write more about. There are many funny, touching, and amazing stories in daily papers. Tonight, I noticed two stories in my local newspaper that I will cut out. Their headlines are, "Chickens stand on guard for our nation," and "Belting bus driver brightens up day," (about a bus driver who serenades his passengers all day.) What great ideas for story characters!

You can also supply your students with a big pile of newspapers and let them find their own poem ideas. If you do that, discuss appropriateness of selected stories—all stories need to be acceptable in a classroom situation. You may even want to mention that you prefer only stories of a humorous or adventurous nature and that you will not approve stories with unacceptable levels of violence as sources for poems.

Mention to students that they may have to search for quite a while before finding a usable story. This activity can encourage them to start reading newspapers and magazines at home to find suitable stories.

Another source for usable news story ideas is the USA Today website. This site has a section already marked "Weird News" at **http://www.usatoday.com/news/nweird.htm**.

The following is an excerpt from a featured article:

> **Deer found taking bubble bath**
> When a couple awoke to strange noises, they thought high winds were rattling their home. What they found was even more unexpected: A deer was taking a bubble bath in their tub. The deer burst through the front door, ran past the couple's bedroom and into the bathroom, somehow managing to turn on the water in the tub and knocking over a bottle of bubble bath. He then submerged himself in the frothy water.

I definitely can see writing a poem about a deer taking a bubble bath.

Keep all suitable newspaper articles in a magnetic photo album for students to use. This protects the paper from yellowing and tearing. Articles I have saved include the following, apparently true, stories. Note how the questions that follow each story help flesh out a poem idea. The article serves as the bones; the questions put meat on the bones! Here are a couple of stories and the kinds of questions to ask.

## Kids find prehistoric egg

This article describes how some children were digging in the dirt, just outside their town, and found a dinosaur egg. According to the report, the children sold the egg to a museum for thousands of dollars.

- The story possibilities are many. Discuss with your students:
- What if it was you who found a dinosaur egg?

- What would you do with it?
- What if you could hatch that dinosaur egg? (In stories, anything is possible).
- Could you write a poem about a dinosaur? Or a poem about a child hatching a dinosaur egg?

## Teens stranded on island for three weeks

This report tells of three teenagers who took their canoe out on a huge lake. They stopped at a little island and, while they were there, their canoe drifted away. The children were presumed drowned, but in reality they lived stranded on the tiny island for three weeks before being rescued.

Here are some questions to ask your students to answer:

- What if that had happened to you and your best friends?
- What would you do? What would you eat? How would you feel?
- How would your friendships change?
- Could you write a poem about loneliness or about the things you'd miss?

Dogs are featured in many interesting articles, as demonstrated by some of the other articles I have:

- A dog that is trained to dial 9-1-1 when his owner needs medical help
- A dog that swallowed a cell phone and was heard "ringing" when the number was dialed
- A goose that frequents a schoolyard to play with the children and barks like a dog
- A Chihuahua in Alaska that was carried off by a bald eagle
- A stray dog that found a lost little boy in the woods, kept him warm, and barked until the rescuers found him

You get the idea: so many wonderful true stories, just waiting to be turned into poetry by your students!

# A Few More Thoughts to Share . . .

- If your classroom situation allows it, whenever your students are engaged in a writing activity, please write along with the kids. There is no stronger message than modeling what you want them to do. If you tell your students how important poetry is and then sit down to do some grading, your good intentions will fall flat. Please write and indulge in the joy of poetry yourself. Don't be embarrassed to share your writing, your thoughts, and your sentiments with the students. There is no lesson more powerful than having them see that you like to write, that you like their writing and that, sometimes, you cry about a memory! Your participation will forge strong bonds between you and your fellow poets.

- When you and your students are sharing poems, please don't make each student get up and read aloud. This can cause some kids to "hate" poetry! Only let those students read aloud who want to. Offer that you or someone else can read a reluctant student's writing or don't share it aloud at all. Students reluctant to read their poems aloud might warm up to the sharing idea later as they gain confidence in their writing abilities.

- As your students complete poems, store them in a binder or file folder for future editing and/or publishing.

- Before your students start writing, stress that they should focus on writing what they want to say and not to stop to worry about neatness, spelling, grammar, or punctuation. At this stage of development, the focus during the creative writing process should be on conveying the intended message or sounds. Students should realize that they are in charge of crafting the poem. They can edit their writing after they complete the first draft. Editing will improve their writing, but it is more important (for now) to be creative and to let their imaginations soar.

# Chapter 2: Bibliography and Websites

## BIBLIOGRAPHY

Bagert, Brod. *Rainbows, Head Lice, and Pea-Green Tile: Poems in the Voice of the Classroom Teacher.* Gainesville, Fla.: Maupin House Publishing, 1999.

Baker, Jeannie. *Window.* Walker Books, 2002.

Banyai, Istvan. *Zoom.* Puffin, 1998.

Base, Graeme. *The Eleventh Hour.* Don Mills, Ont.: Stoddart Publishing, 1988.

Base, Graeme. *The Sign of the Seahorse: A Tale of Greed and High Adventure in Two Acts.* New York: Harry N. Abrams, 1992.

Base, Graeme. *The Water Hole.* New York: Harry N. Abrams, 2001.

Base, Graeme. *The Worst Band in the Universe.* Toronto: Doubleday Canada, 1999.

Booth, David. *Images of Nature: Canadian Poets and the Group of Seven.* Toronto: Kids Can Press, 1995.

Brown, Marc. *Scared Silly! A Book for the Brave.* Boston: Little Brown and Co., 1994.

Burleigh, Robert. *Hoops.* San Diego: Harcourt Brace, 1997.

Fitch, Sheree. *Toes in My Nose: And Other Poems.* Toronto: Doubleday Canada, 1987.

Franco, Betsy. *Math Poetry, Linking Language & Math in a Fresh Way*, Good Year Books, 2006.

Franco, Betsy. *Mathematickles.* Perfection Learning, 2006.

Goforth, Frances S. *Literature & the Learner.* Belmont, Cali.: Wadsworth, 1997.

Goldstein, Bobbye S. *What's on the Menu?* New York: Viking Juvenile, 1992.

Granfield, Linda. *High Flight: A Story of World War II*, Tundra, *1999.*

Granfield, Linda. *In Flanders Fields: The Story of the Poem by John McCrae.* Fitzhenry & Whiteside, 2005.

Granfield, Linda. *Amazing Grace: The Story of the Hymn.* Tundra, 2001.

Hopkins, Lee Bennett. *Dinosaurs.* Orlando: Harcourt Brace, 1987.

Hopkins, Lee Bennett. *Extra Innings: Baseball Poems.* New York: Harcourt, 1993.

Hopkins, Lee Bennett. *Got Geography*. Greenwillow Books, 2006.

Hopkins, Lee Bennett. *Spectacular Science.* Simon & Schuster, 2002.

Jarrell, Randall. *The Bat-Poet.* New York: HarperCollins, 1997.

Kellogg, Steven. *Aster Aardvark's Alphabet Adventures.* New York: Morrow Junior Books, 1987.

Kellogg, Steven. *There Was an Old Woman.* New York: Four Winds, 1981.

Knowles, Sheena. *Edward the Emu.* New York: HarperCollins, 1998.

Korman, Gordon, and Bernice Korman. *The D- Poems of Jeremy Bloom: A Collection of Poems About School, Homework, and Life.* New York: Scholastic, 1992.

Korman, Gordon, and Bernice Korman. *The Last Place Sports Poems of Jeremy Bloom: A Collection of About Winning, Losing, and Being a Good Sport (Sometimes).* New York: Scholastic, 1996.

Lansky, Bruce. *Poetry Party*. New York: Meadowbrook Press, 1996.

Lee, Dennis. *Alligator Pie.* Toronto: Macmillan of Canada, 1974.

Lee, Dennis. *Jelly Belly.* Toronto: Macmillan of Canada, 1983.

Lee, Dennis. *The Ice Cream Store.* New York: HarperCollins, 1991.

Lewis, J. Patrick. *Scien-Trickery: Riddles in Science.* Orlando: Silver Whistle, 2004.

Little, Jean. *I Know an Old Laddie.* New York: Viking Children's Books, 1999.

Martin Jr., Bill, and John Archambault. *Barn Dance!* New York: Henry Holt, 1986.

Mathis, Sharon Bell. *Red Dog Blue Fly, Football Poems.* New York: Viking Children's Books, 1991.

Mortenson, Greg. *Listen to the Wind*. Dial, 2009.

Ormerod, Jan. *Sunshine*. Frances Lincoln, 2009.

Pomerantz, Charlotte. *If I Had a Paka.* New York: Greenwillow Books, 1993.

Prelutsky, Jack. *Something Big Has Been Here.* New York: Scholastic, 1992.

Reid, Barbara. *Two by Two.* Toronto: North Winds Press, 1992.

Remkiewicz, Frank. *Scien-Trickery: Riddles in Science.* Sandpiper, 2007.

Ruurs, Margriet. *In My Backyard.* Toronto: Tundra Books, 2007.

Ruurs, Margriet. *Virtual Maniac: Silly and Serious Poems for Kids.* Gainesville, Fla.: Maupin House Publishing, 2000.

Schertle, Alice. *A Lucky Thing.* New York: Harcourt, 1999.

Schiltz, Laura Amy. *Good Masters! Sweet Ladies! Voices from a Medieval Village.* Somerville, Mass.: Candlewick, 2008.

Service, Robert. *The Best of Robert Service.* Toronto: McGraw Hill, 1971.

Service, Robert. *The Cremation of Sam McGee.* Toronto: Kids Can Press, 2006.

Seuss, Dr. *I Can Read with My Eyes Shut.* New York: Random House, 1978.

Seuss, Dr., and Jack Prelutsky. *Hooray for Diffendoofer Day!* New York: Knopf Books for Young Readers, 1998.

Scieszka, John and Lane Smith. *Science Verse.* Viking, 2004.

Silverstein, Shel. *Falling Up.* New York: HarperCollins, 1996.

Spinelli, Eileen. *Polar Bear, Arctic Hare: Poems of the Frozen North.* Honnesdale, Penn.:Wordsong Press, 2007.

Tang, Greg. *Math-terpieces.* Scholastic, 2003.

Tang, Greg. *Grapes of Math.* Scholastic, 2004.

Viorst, Judith. *The Alphabet from Z to A (With Much Confusion on the Way).* New York: Atheneum, 1994.

Weidt, Maryann N. *Oh, the Places He Went.* Minneapolis: Carolrhoda Books, 1994.

Yolen, Jane. *Best Witches, Poems for Halloween.* New York: G.P. Putnam's Sons, 1989.

## WEBSITES

For more uses of newspapers in the classroom, visit NIEonline: **http://www.nieonline.com**.

For unusual events that can spark stories or poems, go to USA Today's Weird News section: **http://www.usatoday.com/news/offbeat/default.htm**.

# Writing Activities

## Prewriting Activity 1 — Wordstorming!

> The aims of this activity are to generate a wide selection of words and to expand vocabulary.

Exposing students to language in its broadest sense will provide them with a wider word choice once they start writing their own pieces. The child who has not been read to, or who has not been provided with many books before entering school, will find it especially beneficial to listen to, and to discuss, writing possibilities prior to the actual act of composing a poem. Word storming will allow any writer to grasp a wide range of topics and choice of language.

Introduce students to word storming by asking them for a topic. Explain that you will then discuss words that come to mind—any words that are associated to this topic.

You can choose any topic at all. Here are a few to help you get started:

- weather
- holidays
- music
- people
- food

These are pretty broad topics. So you can get more specific if you want:

- sunshine
- beach
- a piano
- my best friend
- chocolate

Decide on your topic and write it on the board. Let's say we chose "chocolate" (my favorite!). Now, ask your students to wordstorm. Which words come to mind when they try to describe chocolate? Write down all responses: brown, yummy, hard, sweet, melting, sharing, mouthwatering. When they seem to run out of descriptive words, start asking questions that will generate more words. For example:

- What does it look like when it melts? (e.g. brown mud, flowing liquid, like my skin, decadent)
- What does it taste like when you take a bite? (e.g. forbidden fruit, heavenly, so sweet, scrumptious, luscious, velvety, smooth)

Keep asking questions and prodding for more words until the well runs dry! Record all words. Once your board is covered in words and students' vocabularies start to be depleted, invite them to write poems using some of the words on the board. If your students have never written poetry, you may want to offer the choice of writing a poem or a short story. But you'll be amazed to see how they use these wordstorms.

A fun online tool to accompany wordstorming is Wordle (**www.wordle.net**). Using words that you either input manually or tell it to pull from another website, Wordle creates a "word cloud"—a graphic representation of those words with customizable fonts, colors, and designs.

Wordstorm often. The activity will increase your students' vocabularies and open their eyes to the possibilities of a poem. When students have written a poem or a short story, ask them to share their writing out loud so others can hear what they did with the words—the same words they all heard. The variety of how they use these same words will be amazing. Once your students get used to the concept of wordstorming, they can start to suggest their own topics to wordstorm.

# Prewriting Activity 2 — Generating Ideas

> The aim of this activity is to help students realize they have stories to tell—from their everyday lives, the books they have read, and more.

An idea is the first thing you need when you want to write. What will you write about? The "idea" is perhaps the most important part of the poem. Without ideas, there wouldn't be poems or story lines. So, it's important to explore the "getting ideas" stage of the writing process.

When a student is assigned the task of writing a poem—or a story for that matter—where does he or she find an idea for what to write about? When I visit a school, the most frequently asked questions are, "Where do you get your ideas?" "Where do ideas come from?" and "How can I help students generate ideas?"

Start off by talking about the importance of keeping track of ideas. Suggest to your students that they use a specific scribbler, a binder, or any kind of notebook dedicated to keeping track of ideas. Encourage them to jot down ideas whenever and wherever they get them: on the school bus, in class, at home, just before falling asleep, etc. I keep a pen with a built-in little light next to my bed, just to record those great ideas that sneak in at night!

Ask your students to start a new page or sheet of paper and write the heading "Ideas" on it. Invite them to jot down any ideas they get while you talk. Show them how to jot down two or three words to help them remember a particular idea. A notation can be as short as "finding a dinosaur egg" or "going to the pool"—just enough to help the student remember that good idea when the time comes to write the poem itself. Discussions with your students about where to get ideas might include the following:

- From reading books of poetry. Reading one poem can trigger ideas for a different poem about a similar topic, but never copy a poem.
- From a movie or TV show. Write your idea down or it will be gone by the time the show is over.
- From your dreams. Try to recall the story you dreamt or use fragments of dreams in your writing.
- From something that actually happened to you. It is a good idea to write about something you know. If you really went skiing, maybe you can write a ski poem, a snow poem, or a cold poem. If you went on an airplane, can you write a poem about traveling, flying, clouds, a suitcase, or a foreign country?
  I traveled on an airplane once and wrote a poem about clouds. Later, it was published in an airline magazine for kids. Another time I was waiting in the airport of Medicine Hat, Alberta, when a cat rubbed up against my suitcase. When I asked what a cat was doing in the airport, I was told that he lived there; they even called him "our airport cat." So, I wrote a poem called "The Airport Cat of Medicine Hat" and it was published too. Maybe you really have a dog. Why not write a poem about him?
- From something someone says. Someone may say one funny word that you might want to write a poem about. Or, they might say something that will give you a complete story idea. Little kids are

especially great at saying funny things that can be turned into poems. If your students have younger brothers or sisters or if they babysit, your students can listen to the funny things the younger kids say. I have a whole notebook full of funny things my own kids said when they were little. Things like :

- "I was born in a hopsetall."
- Pointing to the stamp of the Queen of England on a parcel that came in the mail, my son said, "It's from Grandma! Grandma put her picture on it!"
- "Why is a dragonfly called a dragonfly? Can it breathe fire?"
- "Where does the white go when the snow melts?"

# Prewriting Activity 3 — Generating Ideas: "What If . . ."

> The aims of this activity are to generate ideas and to help students realize their sense of imagination.

Two simple words can spark a multitude of ideas. Ask, "What if . . . ?" and the range of poem possibilities becomes endless.

Use the following books as examples when discussing each subject:

- What if . . . wolves could talk? (*Little Red Riding Hood*)
- What if . . . you were in a plane crash and had to survive on your own in the wilderness? (*Hatchet* by Gary Paulsen)
- What if . . . you met a ghost? (*Awake and Dreaming* by Kit Pearson)
- What if . . . a mitten could keep animals warm in the winter? (*The Mitten* by Jan Brett)
- What if . . . you turned out to be a princess? (*A Royal Pain* by Ellen Conford)

Along with the following prompts, read *What If?* by Laura Vaccaro Seeger. Discuss with your students how real events may lead to poetry when imagination is added.

**TIP:** While brainstorming with your students, remind them to write down their poem ideas while you talk!

- What if . . . you got to go to Disneyland?
- What if . . . you met a movie star?
- Perhaps you really have a horse. What if . . . you won a race?
- Maybe you really have a dog. What if . . . he rescued a child?
- Maybe you really went downhill skiing. What if . . . you witness a mysterious person near a cabin in the backcountry?

Ask your students to make their own "What If" list. These ideas will be in addition to the "Ideas" list they made before. Keep the lists handy for when your students start to write.

Now that they have a supply of wonderful ideas from which to choose, let's start writing poems.

## Writing Activity 1 — Inside Me

> The aim of this activity is to help students use personal thoughts and feelings as inspiration for writing.

A great way to start off the school year (or to get to know students if you are the substitute teacher) is to ask students to write about who they are as an "Inside Me" poem. Explain to them that there is more inside them than organs and blood. What makes them tick? What gets them excited? What do they do outside school? Are they passionate about sports or music? Who are their family members? What are their dreams, their aspirations?

You might want to introduce yourself to the students by writing your own

"Inside Me" poem prior to this session. Write your "Inside Me" poem from the heart, while focusing on what you like and dislike. Forget about trying to be the best poet in the world. Forget about all the writing rules you know! Write from the heart, and then share your poem with the kids.

Now invite the students to tell you about themselves in a poem called "Inside Me" or "What I'm All About." Explain to them that their poems can rhyme or not rhyme. Poems need not rhyme to be poems! (By the way, did you know that there is such a thing as rhyming dictionary? You can use one to find rhyming ends to words. Instead of looking up the first letters of a word, you look for similar-sounding endings. Look for a rhyming dictionary in the library or bookstore and see if you or your students find it helpful in writing poetry.)

Here are two student examples of "Inside Me" poems.

## Inside Me

*Inside me, I'm with old friends*
*singing and laughing, having fun.*
*Inside me, I'm playing outside*
*swinging on a swing, playing soccer.*
*Inside me, the sun shines every day.*
*Later I'm alone again but that's okay*
*Any day with my friends is a perfect day.*

(Natalie, age nine)

## Inside Me

*Inside me there is fun*
*I like to play sports and I like to run.*
*There is snow inside of me. I don't think about the past.*
*I like to live every day as if it were my last.*

(Jeremy, grade 6)

You will notice that, even though I gave the students a topic and title, they were free to decide what about them is important and what aspect of themselves they wanted to talk about. Sharing these poems in the classroom might show a completely different side to their fellow students.

However, please don't ever force a student to share his or her writing. Writing, especially writing poetry, can be a very private activity. Students should always be able to elect not to read out loud.

## Writing Activity 2 — "What If..."

> The aims of this activity are to stimulate
> the students' imaginations and to increase
> their awareness of storytelling.

Some "What If" poems to share with your students include:

- "What If..." by Isabel Joshlin Glaser, from *Dinosaurs*
- "If I Were the Teacher" by Margriet Ruurs, from *Virtual Maniac*
- "If You Should Meet" by Dennis Lee, from *Alligator Pie*

Ask your students to take out their "What If" lists. Those two magical words can be very helpful if you want to write poetry. Ask your students to pick one of their ideas to write a poem about. Or, they can write a poem with an opening sentence that starts with "What if..." Encourage them to let their imaginations run wild while writing this poem!

The "What Ifs" might include:

- What if you won a million dollars...
- What if you could go to the moon...
- What if lollipops grew on trees...

- What if you tripped a bank robber . . .

Allow approximately thirty minutes for students to decide on their topic and write the first draft of their poems. Invite students to read their poems aloud for other students to hear. This will generate more ideas for the next writing period.

## Writing Activity 3 — Tongue Twisters and Nonsense

> The aim of this activity is to demonstrate specific use of language.

This is a fun activity to start off your school year with poetry and to excite students about playing with language. Reading tongue twisters can lead to writing your own! From your book display, choose samples of silly tongue twisters, such as:

- "A Magic Chant," by Bobbi Katz, from *Scared Silly!*
- "The Blug in the Plug," by Sheree Fitch, from *Toes in My Nose*
- "Jilliky Jolliky Jelliky Jee," by Jack Prelutsky, from *Ride a Purple Pelican*
- "Peter Ping and Patrick Pong" by Dennis Lee, from *The Ice Cream Store*
- *Six Sick Sheep: 101 Tongue Twisters* by Joanna Cole and Stephanie Calmensen

Once they have heard lots of fun language, invite the students to choose their favorite letter of the alphabet or to use the first letter of their name. Have them write a list of words that begin with that letter. The list should include nouns and verbs.

Now invite students to compose a tongue twister using most of the words. The tongue twisters can either rhyme or not rhyme.

# Blue Drew

*Drew blew a blue picture and blew blue bubble gum*
*He wore a bright blue sweater that reached down to his bum*

(Natalie, grade 4)

# Silly Sally

*Silly singing Sally sat on a swing*
*singing a super silly song!*

(Chelsey, grade 5)

Reading the tongue twisters out loud gives the children a wonderful taste of poetry. They discover that playing with words is fun, and that they can do it! Making silly tongue twisters that make others laugh gives them a sense of power: word power! They'll enjoy the sounds and the wordplay. They start to realize that any form of rhythmic language is poetry and marvel at it. They'll find joy in discovering words and rhythms.

After having written and shared short tongue twisters, you might want to read a longer, epic poem that celebrates nonsense words, such as:

- *Jabberwocky* by Lewis Carroll
- "The Quangle Wangle's Hat" by Edward Lear, from *The Complete Nonsense of Edward Lear*
- *The Whingdingdilly* by Bill Peet
- *Yertle the Turtle* by Dr. Seuss

Assign your students to write more tongue twisters as they become inspired by the language in these poems. After I read *Jabberwocky* to a group of students, Jackie wrote this poem:

# My Trull is So Drab

*My trull is so drab*
*the drabbest drull*
*you ever saw*
*My bull is sob*
*the sabbest bull you ever saw*

(Jackie, grade 7)

# Writing Activity 4 — Awesome Alliteration

> The aim of this activity is to increase
> poetry-writing skills through alliteration.

Here are some poems that use alliteration:

- *Aster Aardvark's Alphabet Adventures* by Steven Kellogg
- "The Meal" by Karla Kuskin, from *What's on the Menu?*
- "Moose Meadow" by Margriet Ruurs, from *Virtual Maniac*
- "The Pig in Pink Pajamas" by Dennis Lee, from *The Ice Cream Store*
- "Snowflake Soufflé" by X. J. Kennedy, from *For Laughing Out Loud*
- "A Vote For Vanilla" by Eve Merriam, from *What's on the Menu?*

In the previous activity, students experienced the fun of working with sounds. Let's broaden their options and introduce them to the technique of alliteration. Explain to your students that using words beginning with the same sounds is alliteration. Write a list of examples on the board and solicit more suggestions from the students. Be sure to include alliteration made by both beginning vowels as well as consonants. The following are some examples:

- big brown bear
- mountain magic

- the terrible twos
- eight elegant elephants
- the sun set slowly
- shine and shade
- flying flamingos

You can also make a list of name alliterations for characters in later poems. Some suggestions:

- Wild Willy of the West
- Principal Peters
- Miss Muffins
- Silly Simon
- Jumping Jack

You could even come up with an alliteration for each letter of the alphabet. For instance, an animal alphabet:

A – amazing alligators
B – big brown bears
C – crazy crocodile
D – dancing dogs

For more ideas, see:

- *Animal Alphabed* by Margriet Ruurs (This is a continuous story using alliterations and all letters of the alphabet)
- *A Mountain Alphabet* by Margriet Ruurs (This is a book of nonfiction about the mountain environment)
- *A Pacific Alphabet* by Margriet Ruurs (A book of alliteration and rhyming poems about the Pacific coast)

Now ask your students to write a poem using any of the listed alliterations or to invent new ones to write a perfect poem! Have fun sharing them.

# Writing Activity 5 — Rhythm and Rhyme

> The aim of this activity is to increase poetry-writing skills through awareness of rhythm and rhyme.

Even though poetry need not rhyme in order to be poetry, kids love writing poems that rhyme! However, when they write rhyming poems, the words tend to take them in a direction that they may not have intended to write about. They will write about "a mouse who lived in a house" not because they want to write about a mouse, but simply because it rhymes with house. I like to stress to them that they should focus on the story they want to tell and then find rhyming words that suit the story. I tell them, "You are the boss of this poem; you make the words do what you want them to do!"

Here are some techniques that help generate rhyme:

It is easy to find words that rhyme if you remove the first letter of the word and substitute another letter of the alphabet until the letters make a suitable word. For example:

band        hand        land        sand

Write commonly used words, such as the following, on the board and ask students to find a rhyming word for each:

head        dog        boy        home        scared

tear        house        happy        car        train

Now ask the students to pick some of these words and write a rhyming poem with them.

You can also switch the words of a sentence around to find a better word to rhyme with. If the line that you want to rhyme with is,

"all night the dog barked"

and you can't find a word to rhyme with "barked," maybe you can change the sentence around to say,

"the dog barked all night"

Now you can rhyme with "right" or "fight." You could also change the sentence so that it says,

"all the dog did was bark"

and now you can rhyme with "dark," "shark," or "park."

# Writing Activity 6 — Painting Pictures with Words

> The aim of this activity is to increase writing skills through appropriate use of language.

Kids often think that if it doesn't rhyme, it isn't poetry. Discovering that poetry need not rhyme can bring a kind of freedom to a young author. Since rhyming tends to take students in a different direction from the intended story, experimenting with non-rhyming poetry frees them to concentrate on what they really want the poem to say. Emphasize to your students that they are in charge of the words, not the other way around. They need to choose words that "paint the right picture." The target, when painting mind pictures, is to make someone else (the reader) feel what you (the writer) feel. Using the right words helps to accomplish that.

This activity helps students understand that poems need not rhyme. Start by reading a variety of non-rhyming poetry, such as:

- *Hoops* by Robert Burleigh
- "The Ocean" by Margriet Ruurs, from *Virtual Maniac*
- *Owl Moon* by Jane Yolen
- "Poor Ron's Allergy" by Brod Bagert, from *Let Me Be the Boss*
- "Quiet Storm" by Lydia Okutoro, from *Quiet Storm*
- "The Wind of Spring" by Myra Cohn Livingston, from *Make Things Fly*

This activity makes children aware of how poetry differs from prose visually and of the specific choices of words and patterns in poetry. Have them rewrite any poem in their own words as a story; then consider how the two ways of telling the story differ. This practice helps them experience what makes a poem: shorter sentences, rhythmic and condensed language, and sometimes rhyme— but not necessarily.

Let's do this as a group activity with the whole class.

**STEP 1**. Use the following poem:

# Campfire Time

*The crackling campfire dances*
*with long, licking flames,*
*while we sing silly songs and*
*play a million games.*

*Snapping, crackling twigs*
*compete with blazing fire*
*as glowing firefly sparks*
*dance higher and higher.*

*Teasing, threatening,*
*golden tongues lick*
*at the dark of night*
*and at my marshmallow stick.*

(Margriet Ruurs, from *Virtual Maniac*)

Write down the poem so all students can see your demonstration lesson. Read it aloud with the students.

**STEP 2**. Now ask them to tell you what is happening and record the event as a story, like a reporter who was there to observe. Prod them with questions if need be (Where? When? Who? What?).

This kind of description will emerge:

It was nighttime. A group of people were sitting around a campfire. They were singing and telling stories. The fire was making noise and sending off sparks. They were also roasting marshmallows.

**STEP 3**. Examine how the two accounts differ with the following techniques:

- Point out the use of shorter lines in the poem. Even if one whole verse is one sentence, it has been broken into shorter chunks.
- Find the places where the technique of alliteration was used in the poem. Did we use alliteration in the description?
- Determine the rhyme scheme of the poem.
- Discuss which account paints a better picture in your head.

**STEP 4**. Since this poem happens to rhyme, let's rewrite it as a non-rhyming poem to demonstrate that it will still be poetry:

## Campfire Time

*Crackling campfire dances*
*with long, licking flames*
*as we sit under the blanket of night*
*and try counting stars in the sky.*

*Snapping, crackling twigs*
*compete with blazing fire*
*as glowing sparks dance*
*their own campfire song.*

*Teasing, threatening,*
*golden tongues*
*lick at the black of night*
*and lap up the darkness.*

**STEP 5**. Compare the rhyming and the non-rhyming versions of the poem. Which do you prefer? Why? How do their sounds differ? Do they paint different pictures?

**STEP 6**. Invite your students to write their own non-rhyming poem. They can try to rewrite a rhyming poem they wrote previously, or they can decide to write a non-rhyming poem about any topic: nature, a memory, something funny, something sad, a place, a person, anything at all!

Showing them these different versions will emphasize the importance of editing and rewriting. Don't erase your first draft! If you do, you can't see how a piece of writing grows and develops.

If they need help coming up with a topic to write about, you can supply pictures from your picture file, suggest a recent event or experience, or ask your students to describe their pet or to have a look at their "Idea" or "What If . . . ?" lists.

Here is one of my favorite non-rhyming poems, written by a fourth grader:

## First Snow

*One morning as I awoke*
*I looked outside and saw*
*the first snow had come*
*like a great cloud of white*
*settled over the country.*
*It was early morning*
*no footprints in the snow*
*Just a velvet carpet of white.*
*I got up, hurried to be the first*
*to jump and roll and make my impression.*
*It was cold outside*
*but that did not matter*
*It had snowed*
*That's what mattered.*

(Emily, age nine)

# Writing Activity 7 — Nature Poetry

> The aims of this activity are to increase
> vocabulary and to write from memory.

Here are some nature poems to read with your students:

- "Aska's Animals" by David Day and Warabé Aska
- "Eons, Hours, and Wind" by Brod Bagert, from *Let Me Be the Boss*
- "Owl Moon" by Jane Yolen
- "Owls in the Wood" by Margriet Ruurs, from *Virtual Maniac*
- "The Wind was on the Withered Heath" by J. R. R. Tolkien, from *The Magic Tree*

After sharing such poems by your favorite authors, ask your students to write some nature poems. Invite your students to close their eyes and recall a special place they know and to write about that spot:

- a wintry trail on a snowy hill
- a spot in the sun by a sparkling river
- a sturdy branch of a tree they like to sit in
- an icy sidewalk
- snow in your backyard or school ground

Ask them to really concentrate on that place by using all their senses: sound, smell, touch, taste, and sight. You may need to spend ten minutes or so talking about the scenes and the possibilities. Try to create a relaxed, quiet atmosphere.

Now, invite the students to write a poem about the place they pictured in their head. Urge them not to worry about correct spelling or grammar rules. It is important to focus on the essence of the story line.

If they have trouble thinking of such a place or event, supply them with pictures of nature paintings. I use pictures that show animals and flowers in mountain settings, photos of farm animals, a flower in bloom, dew drops on the grass, and so on.

Taking your class out into nature— such as a field trip or even just under a tree on the school grounds— may motivate good nature poems.

If your classroom situation allows, participate in the activity by writing your own poem. Let the children write for as long as the majority can remain quiet. When most are done, invite the students to share. You might want to start off by reading the poem you wrote or by offering to read a particularly well-written poem by a shy student who volunteers. It won't be long before they'll be eager to share their writing.

Follow-up activities might include painting an illustration to accompany the poem. Pictures and poems can be displayed on a wall.

### Blue Flower
*Blue flower growing in a corn field,*
*you look so out of place*
*Growing in a field of gold*
*you hold up your head with grace.*

(Tara, grade 6)

# Writing Activity 8 — Music is Poetry

> The aim of this activity is to create awareness
> of language use in lyrics.

All songs are poems. If you take away the tune, you are left with the lyrics.

Lyrics make wonderful, often rhyming, poetry. Listen to songs in your classroom by bringing in a CD player or an iPod. You might want to select a few good examples ahead of time, such as:

- "Baby Beluga" by Raffi
- "Heal The World" by Michael Jackson
- "The Sporting Life" by the Decemberists
- "Yesterday" by the Beatles
- "Drive" by Incubus
- "The Littlest Birds" by the Be Good Tanyas

Picking age-appropriate lyrics from popular artists such as Beyoncé and Justin Timberlake can be effective examples in your classroom, as can classics from artists such as Elton John and Paul Simon. Additionally, the text of the songs from certain Disney movies, such as *The Lion King* and *Tangled* are very cleverly crafted; so are songs from musicals, such as "The Music of the Night" from *The Phantom of the Opera*.

**STEP 1**. Select a song with good lyrics. Listen to the entire song once with your students, then play the song again and stop the tape at short intervals so that your students can listen to the text. Ask a few students to record the words on paper or hand out copies of the lyrics.

**STEP 2**. Read the song as a poem. How is it different when spoken? Which parts of the text had they picked up on already? Which rhyming words did they notice?

You may want to ask students to bring in a favorite piece of music. They will enjoy listening to their own music and choosing their favorite lyrics to share with the class.

**STEP 3**. Ask your students to pick a poem they have written, or invite them to write a poem specifically for this activity. When the poem is completed, try to put it to a tune. They can select their own favorite genre. One student may want to hum his or her song to a country tune.

Others might want to get together and rap their poem.

Students could be teamed up to produce songs and perform them. As an example of how poems can be put to music, show your students the book *Ride a Purple Pelican* by Jack Prelutsky. Get the taped version of this book from your library to hear how each poem is presented as a song. A wide variety of tunes is used to sing each poem.

# Writing Activity 9 — And Poetry is Music!

> The aims of this activity are to write creatively and to increase poetry skills.

Instrumental music works well in inspiring children to write. Setting the mood for this writing activity is very important. Ask students to get into a comfortable position in their chairs or on the floor. Create a cozy, relaxed atmosphere in the classroom by closing blinds or dimming fluorescent lights.

Make sure students are equipped with paper and pencils that won't need sharpening for a while. Play quiet, instrumental music. Selections can include instrumental versions of Broadway shows, movie soundtracks, or classical music by Tchaikovsky, Strauss, and Mozart.

Ask students to listen to the music, and to let the music start to paint a picture in their minds. Then they can start writing a poem about the scene they see in their heads while listening to the music. Make the activity last for as long as the students' attention spans will keep them listening and writing.

Here's a poem one seventh grader wrote while listening to instrumental music:

# Flamingos

*An unfolded treasure blooming in sparkling water,*
*silky flowers bursting from a deep sleep,*
*Magical rose crayons scribble on swift paper,*
*light flamingos dance under the tender moon.*

(Tara, grade 7)

# Writing Activity 10 — Poems That Tell Stories

> The aim of this activity is to learn
> narrative writing skills.

Books/poems to read include:

- "The Cremation of Sam McGee" by Robert Service
- "The Eleventh Hour" by Graeme Base
- *The Party* by Barbara Reid
- *The Sign of the Seahorse* by Graeme Base
- "Stopping By Woods on a Snowy Evening" by Robert Frost
- *There's a Mouse in My House* by Sheree Fitch

Read one of the suggested narrative poems above and discuss the elements that make it different from a descriptive poem (which does not tell a story but paints a picture or evokes a feeling). Discuss the beat of the poem. Listen for the beat. Read the verses in an exaggerated manner and have the kids clap their hands to the beat.

After you have shared epic poems such as "The Cremation of Sam McGee" and "The Eleventh Hour" with your students, ask them to write their own "story poem"—a tale told in rhyme format. Share the poems through classroom readings. Topics/titles can include:

- "The Ballad of [your school name]"
- "The Voyage of the Seventh Grade Field Trip"
- Legends such as "How the Tiger Got Its Tail" or
  "How the Zebra Got Its Stripes"

Here is an example of a poem written by one of my students that tells a story:

# Shipwrecked

*I went to an island*
*a long ways away.*
*It remains undiscovered*
*to this very day.*

*I landed on this island.*
*You see, I was shipwrecked*
*on a long sailing voyage*
*as far as I recollect.*

*The ship's name I cannot remember*
*nor any of the crew.*
*I saw no animals*
*so ate leaves and bamboo.*

*Then I found some natives*
*who praised me and called me Zeus.*
*I sat there thinking*
*that I could put this to use.*

*I lived there for some twenty years*
*My story told to few.*
*And I give you this privilege:*
*I tell it now to you.*

(Marcus, grade 7)

# Writing Activity 11 — Metaphor and Simile

> The aim of this activity is to learn the poetry-writing techniques of metaphor and simile.

Poetry is like porridge: it warms the body and the soul. Metaphors and similes can be a strong part of poetry. Kids love using metaphor and simile, often doing so even if they are not familiar with the terms. The concept of metaphor is something they frequently already use unconsciously. Even very young writers who are unfamiliar with the definitions will understand the idea.

Explain to your students that when we compare two things and say they are "like" each other, it is called a simile: "The rain fell like tears." In a metaphor, dissimilar things are compared without the word "like": "The moon was a beckoning lantern."

## METAPHOR

When you write a metaphor, you use your imagination to describe it. You could call a storm "a fierce lion" or a flower "a yellow symphony." In the following poem, I compare the ocean to a dragon, but it's never directly stated.

# The Ocean

*A giant dragon,*
*breathing foam*
*on rocky,*
*green toes.*

*It roars,*
*then softly rumbles,*
*retreats to attack again.*

*It gathers misty breath and strength*
*to roar back with all its might*
*and eat away at sand and caves,*
*its belly softly rumbling.*

*It rests*
*Gray back panting, heaving,*
*rise and fall,*
*it slumbers*
*then wakes again and roars,*
*spitting foam and salty mist.*

(Margriet Ruurs, *Virtual Maniac*)

Brainstorm with your students what other comparisons you could make. Make a list of metaphors on the blackboard. For example:

- My kitten is a powder puff
- Our country is a melting pot
- Icy teeth hung off the roof
- Her eyes were bright diamonds

Now, with the class, make a list of *real* things and then write a metaphor for each word:

SUBJECT:                         METAPHOR:

_____Storm_____          _____Lion_____

_____          _____

_____          _____

_____          _____

_____          _____

_____          _____

Now invite your students to pick one metaphor from these lists and write a metaphor poem!

Here's one of my favorites. Sarah compared the wind to angels in her poem:

# The Wind

*The angels sing their haunting tunes,*
*wailing high and low.*
*They sweep between the maple trees,*
*as on and on they blow.*
*The angels' gray and foggy skirts*
*are dragging through the grass.*
*And as I look out my window,*
*by and by they pass.*

(Sarah, grade 7)

## SIMILE

The following is an example of a simile poem:

### Flying Free

*I know that if I really try,*
*deep down I know that I can fly!*
*Standing on a fence,*
*flapping with my hands,*
*I'll soar through the sky,*
*like a bird I will fly.*

*Floating free as a cloud*
*over treetops I'll sail about,*
*I know that if I really try,*
*deep down I know that I can fly!*
*So, here I go!*

(Margriet Ruurs)

"Like a bird I will fly," the poem says. What other expressions do we use to compare ourselves to animals? Can your students think of some? Write all suggestions down on the blackboard.

Did they think of "quiet as a mouse" or "gentle as a lamb"? We also say, "You swim like a fish" and "He is strong as a bear." Save the list of animal similes you now have for use in future poems.

Invite your students to write down other common similes. Now, ask them to choose one simile and write a poem about it. They might choose to write a poem about being strong as a horse, roaring like a lion, or swimming like a fish!

## "GUESS WHAT?"

It is fun to turn metaphor poetry into a game by writing poems and asking each other to guess what it really is about. Ask your students to think of a subject, and then decide what it is like. This is similar to how I decided that the ocean is like a dragon. If your students need warming up to this activity, discuss more examples, list them on the board, and allow your students to use those. Here are some suggestions:

- Spring could be a butterfly.
- Rain could be tears.
- Worries can be a heavy package or a suitcase.

One of my students wrote about a rainbow, calling it a smile in the sky:

## Rainbow
*Something is way up high*
*an upside-down smile in the sky.*
*After the tears go*
*the upside-down smile starts to glow.*

(Chelsey, grade 4)

To demonstrate the guessing element, read this poem to your students without revealing the title. Ask them to guess what it is about.

Now, ask your students to write their poems— but not to reveal the true subject when sharing. Turn the sharing of the poems into a guessing game by inviting the rest of the class to guess the real topic of each poem!

# Writing Activity 12 — Fortunately Poetry!

> The aim of this activity is to engage
> students' imagination.

Turn poetry writing into a tasty subject. Buy a bag of fortune cookies, enough to have one cookie for each student in your group. This next part is a little tedious, but well worth the effort! With a pair of tweezers, remove the original slip of paper from each fortune cookie and discard. To save time, you can also find blank fortune cookie kits online. Write a short sentence (or just a noun with an adjective) on little slips of paper. The words you choose can be random or you may decide on a theme. Fold and insert one into each fortune cookie.

Have your students break open their cookie and write a poem about the words, starting with the words they find. Delicious poetry will follow.

Use your own imagination to write sentences or use these samples:

- The galloping horse
- Softly falling snow
- The giggling girl
- Gentle lapping water
- The strong man lifted the child
- Which puppy to choose
- A happy smile greeted me
- Six silly sisters
- It shook and it creaked
- The road was windy up ahead
- The cat curled up and…
- The wind howled as…
- Slowly, I opened the book

# Writing Activity 13 — Poetry Workout

> The aim of this activity is to increase students' confidence in their writing skills.

Here is a fun writing activity that will get even the most reluctant student excited about writing. Students can write either poems or short stories with this technique.

What you need:

- a used dictionary (find them at used book sales, garage sales, etc.)
- one sheet of lined paper and one pencil per student
- something to ring at the start and finish (I use a cowbell; you could use any kind of bell—an alarm clock, an egg timer, a horn, a whistle, or even a bicycle bell!)

**STEP 1**. Explain to the students that you are now going to do a "poetry workout." Workouts are meant to exercise your body, but this one will give your brain a workout! Briefly explain the process as it is outlined below. Emphasize to your students that they may not complete a finished piece of writing. Explain that this exercise is merely an activity to have fun with words and to help them discover how well they can write in a very short time. They will be amazed at what they can do! Before proceeding, explain steps two through four with your students.

**STEP 2**. Go around the classroom and let students tear out a page of your used dictionary. Let them pick a page, any page, and rip it out. They immediately have to put their page under their sheet of writing paper, without peeking at it. They should all start at the same time, so reiterate that they should not look at their page yet!

**STEP 3**. Once all students have received a page from the dictionary, you will ring your bell. When the bell rings, students are to take out their ripped page, scan the page for words, and choose any word from their page.

**STEP 4**. At this point, you may have to walk from desk to desk and point out good words. Once the student has decided on his or her word, that word becomes the topic of his or her poem. The student should quickly think about the story he or she wants to tell about this topic—beginning, middle, or end. The student then starts writing, without pausing to worry about spelling or punctuation.

Please note: It is important that they realize they can use any word, not just the bold ones listed in alphabetical order. They can use any word, combination of words, or short phrase of their choice—as long as it appears somewhere on the page, front or back.

**STEP 5**. Allow a reasonable amount of time for this activity based on how long your students remain quiet and focused. This may be as short as ten minutes for grades 3-5 or fifteen minutes for grades 6-8. You can increase the amount of time as you repeat this session and students get used to this form of writing. Ring the bell as the signal for all students to stop writing immediately.

**STEP 6**. Invite students to share with the rest of the group the words they chose and the poems they wrote.

Please note:

- While your students are writing (and if your classroom situation allows it) pick your own page and write your own story or poem along with them! Share it, if you like, and your students will be encouraged by your example— especially if your poem isn't quite perfect!
- Occasionally invite the principal, parents, or anyone else to join the students in this activity and see how much you can accomplish in a short time.

# Writing Activity 14 — Personal Favorites Poetry

> The aim of this activity is to help students use their personal preferences and tastes as inspiration for poetry.

Draw on students' favorite things to encourage the writing of poems.
Ask your students:

- "What is your favorite animal?" Invite students to write a poem without saying outright which animal they wrote about. Can the class guess it? You can also use this technique with other favorites: sports, celebrities, colors, etc.
- "What is your favorite story?" Ask students to write a poem describing their favorite movie or a poem from the perspective or their favorite fictional character.
- "What is your favorite food?" Ask students to pick their favorite food and write a poem about it. It could be about bubblegum ice cream, sloppy soup, crumbly cookies, or their favorite candy!

A fun way to publish personal favorites poetry is by asking your students to make a Glog, an interactive online poster. They can include pictures, designs, and even video along with their poems. Visit **www.edu.glogster.com** to register for a free educator's account.

Have delicious fun! Why not hand out some candy while sharing these poems? Get your class in the mood by reading food poems such as:

- "A Matter of Taste" by Eve Merriam, from *What's on the Menu*
- "Sleeping Dragons All Around" by Sheree Fitch
- "Twickham Tweer" by Jack Prelutsky, from *The Sheriff of Rottenshot*

# Writing Activity 15 — Times of Your Life

> The aim of this activity is to increase the vocabulary
> that deals with feelings and emotions.

Your students' memories will be the source of poetic material for this activity. Ask your students to choose one of the following three options to inspire their "I Remember" poems:

*Option 1: I Remember When...*

- Think back to when you were little.... You can do it if you try hard. Concentrate.... What sort of things do you remember? Things like:
  - What is your earliest memory?
  - What did your bedroom look like?
  - What kind of toys did you have?
  - Do you remember sitting in a car seat? In a stroller?

- Think of a time in your life, and then write a poem about, when you were:
  - very happy
  - scared
  - sad
  - excited

*Option 2: Special to Me*

- Think of a special person and write a poem about him or her.
- Think about place that is special to you. Your bedroom or an old house? The kitchen where your grandmother baked muffins? A tree house? Maybe it's the library or the public pool.
- Do you have any special memories that might make a good poem? Is it visiting a grandma? Or swinging in the playground? Or going on a trip?

*Option 3: The First Time*

- Think of the first time you went somewhere special. Can you remember your first trip to Disneyland? What about the beach or to a school dance?
- Can you remember the first time you met your best friend? What about the first time you got a pet?

Ask your students to decide on a memory and then write a poem about it.

# Writing Activity 16 — Pick a Word, Any Word!

> The aim of this activity is to practice poetry-writing skills by combining nouns and adjectives.

This writing exercise uses words as a starting point. Similar to the "Poetry Workout," this workshop will give students good writing practice while having fun.

You will need:

- multiple pieces of paper with a noun written on each one (a few more than you have students)
- multiple pieces of paper with an adjective written on each one (a few more than you have students)
- two envelopes or decorated sandwich bags
- one piece of lined paper and one pencil per student

Type or print one word clearly on each piece of paper. Choose any kind of noun, for example:

| | | |
|---|---|---|
| backpack | computer | pool |
| New York City | dinosaur | puppy |
| boy | hippopotamus | school |
| Lauren | pirate | racecar |

Now write your adjectives on different pieces of paper. Some examples:

| | | |
|---|---|---|
| barking | giggling | sad |
| curious | large | ugly |
| fast | polka-dotted | wide-eyed |
| funny | purple | wiggly |

Put the pieces of paper with the nouns in one envelope and the pieces of paper with the adjectives in another envelope. Label both envelopes. Review with your students the meaning of "noun" and "adjective." Then give each student a sheet of paper and a pencil.

For variety, you could also make the rule that the two words don't form the title but need to occur somewhere in the poem.

Let each student pick a piece of paper, one from each envelope. The topic of each story or poem comes from combining the pieces of paper. They will end up with funny combinations (such as a "purple dinosaur" or a "barking boy") to write a story or poem about.

Allow a relatively short period of time for students to write fast and furiously. When the students complete the writing process, encourage them to read their writing aloud. You can display the completed, edited writing on a wall, together with the words that were picked.

# Writing Activity 17 — Picture Perfect Poems

> The aim of this activity is to use language appropriate to the format of poetry writing.

This activity uses pictures as a starting point. As suggested in the section in Chapter 2, "Making a Picture File to Generate Ideas," you have hopefully been collecting funny and interesting photographs and illustrations.

Discuss with your students the importance of illustrations in books and how pictures tell their own stories. Ask them to take a close look at the picture they will get from your collection and to write a story that goes with it. Tell them to look for what is happening, what might have just happened, and what might happen next. What is the story in this picture?

Go around with your envelope of pictures and let each student pick one without looking. They should quickly put their pictures under their sheets of paper without peeking.

Once each student has a picture, you can ring your bell (to add to the sense of excitement) as a signal for the kids to take their pictures out.

The kids should look at their pictures, quickly think of a story to tell (beginning, middle and end) and start writing. After the initial excitement, there shouldn't be a lot of talking.

When the bell rings again, students should stop writing immediately. Invite them to share the pictures they picked and the poems they created. Display edited poems with the pictures that prompted each story.

Here is an example based on a picture that showed a museum guard dozing off on the job. A student in one of my writing workshops wrote this poem in about twelve minutes!

## Museum Guard

*I work in the museum,*
*guarding pictures where everyone can see 'em.*
*It's a picture made completely of tiles*
*I think it was made by some guy named Giles,*
*a picture of Romans in robes and sandals*
*and I have to protect it from thieves and vandals.*
*I was standing there, doing what I always do,*
*When I noticed I had to tie up my shoe.*

*Now while I was down there, I did not realize*
*that the picture started rippling,*
*then one of those guys stepped right out, stepped onto the floor*
*I'm sure that's never happened before.*
*In no time he was some distance away*
*and no one knows where he is, to this very day.*
*All I know is I don't have that job anymore.*
*I still work at the museum but now I clean the floor.*

(TaraLynn, grade 7)

# Writing Activity 18 — Words That Paint Pictures

> The aims of this activity are to increase vocabulary
> and poetry-writing skills.

Poets don't use illustrations to make you see what they want you to see. Poets paint pictures with words. In poetry, you can use language and compare things in a way that you wouldn't in prose. Choosing the right words is especially important.

Ask your students to write a poem that really paints a picture in the reader's head. It can be about anything they like, but the more specific the subject, the easier of a time they'll have describing it. When they finish writing, let them read their poems aloud to a classmate; do the words paint a picture in their minds? Editing after the first draft will help your students find even better words and make the image clearer.

## Content Cat

*Pink pussycat nose*
*padded pussycat toes.*
*Swooshy black tail,*
*whiskers that trail,*
*powderpuff fur,*
*a pleased pussycat purr!*

Invite your students to choose one of the poems they have written and to draw a picture to go with it. Drawing before and during the writing process helps your students rough out the story. Drawing is more than just doodling and can serve a real purpose.

# Writing Activity 19 — [Day] Dream Poems

> The aim of this activity is to encourage the use of dreams and imagination in poetry.

*Option 1: Shapes in the Clouds*

Discuss with your students:

- Did you ever lie on your back in the grass to watch the clouds float through the sky? Did you use your imagination to see things or animals in the shapes?

- Close your eyes to remember the shapes or look out of the classroom window to see clouds.
- Write a poem about the clouds. You can write about one cloud and the shapes it makes. Or, you can write about all the different clouds you see in the sky.

# Clouds

*Melted marshmallow puff cloud,*
*floating in air, sailing about.*
*Cotton candy without a stick—*
*can I float up to take a lick?*

*Spoonful of whipping cream,*
*summerday's dream.*
*Can I jump in your lap*
*for a fleeting, float nap?*

*Clouds of soft cottonball fluff,*
*snow white bunnytail puff,*
*can I somersault up high*
*to float with you through the sky?*

*Option 2: Dreaming Poetry*

Discuss with your students:

- That special time between just being awake and falling asleep is often the time you get lots of good ideas floating through your head.
- Do you remember the ideas when you wake up? Do you remember any dreams you had? Were there strange happenings?
- Can you use any dream fragments about which to write poems?

A good poem to read in conjunction with Option 2 is "Keep a Poem in your Pocket" by Beatrice Schenk de Regniers, from *Something Special*.

# Writing Activity 20 — S-e-n-s-ible Poems

> The aims of this activity are to increase awareness
> of senses and to build sensory vocabulary, as well as
> poetry writing skills.

## POEMS YOU CAN SMELL!

Discuss with your students:

- What are your favorite smells? Popcorn? Cookies? Roast beef?
- Do they bring good memories?
- Which smells do you hate? Do they bring bad memories to mind?

Smells can help bring instant pictures to mind. Putting a smell in your poem will create a strong sensory image with which people can identify. If I describe the annual fair in my hometown by saying we have a midway and animal displays, it will take me many more words to make you "see" the fair in your head; but what if I tell you that smells of hotdogs, popcorn, and cotton candy waft around the midway—and that you have to be careful not to step in warm cow pies when you go to see the pink piglets huddled in the sweet-smelling hay?

Think of good smells (muffins, puppies, a damp forest) and bad smells (hospital hallways, burning rubber). Write a poem in which smells are important!

Read "Smelly Poem" by Margriet Ruurs from *Virtual Maniac*.

## A SOUND POEM

Remind your students that poems don't have to rhyme to be poems. Any story told in a rhythmic kind of way–in short sentences, for example—is a poem.

- Let's write a poem with sounds in it: it could be wedding bells or a meowing kitten, a howling wolf or creaking branches.
- Try to write a poem that sounds like an animal. The words could ROAR, or the lines could quietly tiptoe like a mouse.
- Write a quiet or a LOUD poem! Just for fun, read:
  - "I Know All the Sounds That the Animals Make" by Jack Prelutsky, from *Something Big Has Been Here*
  - *Slow Sloth's Slow Song* by Jack Prelutsky, from *Something Big Has Been Here*
  - "Noises" by Danielle Caryl

## FEEL THAT POEM!

Many poems deal with feelings. But did you put real feeling words into the poem? If students write about being scared, their poems will be much stronger if they show they were scared. As you know, the golden rule in writing is to show, don't tell! So, show *scared* by using sentences such as "He felt a thousand invisible eyes on his back; His hair stood on end and prickles ran down his spine" or "She felt her skin tingle as she slowly turned and held her breath in anguish." Wordstorming (see Prewriting Activity 1 on page 36) will help students increase their vocabulary for *scared* words and feelings.

Think of, and discuss, other feelings: *embarrassed, excited, lonely, surprised, frustrated.* Wordstorm and have students write about these feelings in a similar way.

- A good sample of a poem showing *hope* is "To You" by Langston Hughes, from *Soul Looks Back in Wonder*

- A deliciously *scary* poem to recite is "What's That?" by Florence Parry Heide, from *Scared Silly!*

Ask your students to write a "feelings" poem using many words to describe how they feel. Here is a poem that one of my e-mail students wrote using all senses, as well as the wordplay of senses/scents:

## The Scents of Christmas

*The warm smell of chocolaty steam*
*rising from your cocoa.*
*The taste of colorful sprinkles on gingerbread,*
*warming your lips.*
*The feeling of a wool blanket*
*hugging your chilled body*
*sitting comfortably by the fireplace.*
*The sight of presents in shiny paper,*
*the loudness of Christmas spirit surrounding*
*every window of carolers*
*with shining, smiling faces.*

(Kim, grade 8)

After visiting Indonesia, I wanted to use senses to recreate a vivid image of this amazing country. I wrote the following poem, which was published in *Highlights for Children* in July 2010:

## A Sense of Indonesia

*Once you have heard*
*the call for prayer floating on the air,*
*haunting cries of gibbons*
*laughter of hornbills everywhere –*

*Once you have smelled*
*ground spices and dried fish,*
*rain forest's fragrant flowers*
*a warm nasi goreng dish –*

*Once you have felt*
*tropical nights wrap you in a hug,*
*rain pouring on your skin*
*and a kite's upward tug –*

*Once you have seen*
*palm oil plantations without end,*
*children dancing in the rain,*
*wise old eyes of an elephant—*

*Then Indonesia you'll know*
*and you won't want to leave,*
*always dream of coming back*
*to Java, Sumatra, and Borneo.*

Using my poem as an example, students in international schools have written about the places where they have lived or visited. Using different senses, really brings these images to life. Here is another student example:

## South Africa

*You won't know South Africa until you've heard*
*The roar of a lion, the shrill sound of running impala*
*Or the immense yawn of a hippo.*
*You won't know South Africa until you've felt*
*The hot sun beating down on your skin,*
*Or icy nights bringing goose bumps.*
*You won't know South Africa until you've tasted*
*sweet, tender warthog meat dipped in strong, spicy sauce.*
*You won't know South Africa until you've seen*
*A lion family: a mother nursing cubs so they will grow up*
*Strong and healthy, just like her.*

(Sara, grade 6)

# Writing Activity 21 — A Found Poem!

> The aim of this activity is to create awareness of
> the different uses of format in writing.

Just as you can find things that become treasures, you can find words that, put together, make a poem. I'll show you, and you can share this activity in the same way with your students.

Here is a piece of writing:

> When I was little, Grandma's button box was my favorite toy. I would sit on the floor by Grandma's chair and she would bring me the button box. Gently, she'd bend down and put it by my feet on the carpet. Slowly, I'd lift the lid and stare at the treasure. Glittering, shimmering jewels they were: shiny black eyes, golden coins, and sparkling diamonds off princesses' dresses.
>
> Then I'd tilt the box, slowly, with both hands until the buttons poured out onto the carpet. I'd shift them with my hands, let them run through my fingers in a cascade of colors. I'd make piles and bulldoze them around the carpet. I felt the buttons. They felt good.

Now I am going to pick words from this piece of writing and put them into a poem. I will underline the words I choose:

> When I was little, Grandma's button box was my favorite toy. I would sit on the floor by Grandma's chair and she would bring me the button box. Gently, she'd bend down and put it by my feet on the carpet. Slowly, I'd lift the lid and stare at the treasure. Glittering, shimmering jewels

they were: shiny black <u>eyes</u>, golden coins, and <u>sparkling</u> diamonds off princesses' dresses.

Then I'd tilt the box, slowly, with <u>both hands</u> until the buttons poured out onto the carpet. I'd shift them with <u>my hands</u>, let them run through my fingers in a cascade of colors. I'd make piles and bulldoze them around the carpet. I felt the buttons. They <u>felt good</u>.

Now I put these underlined words into a poem. Look:

## Grandma

*I was little*
*Gently*
*her eyes sparkled*
*Both hands*
*in my hands*
*Grandma felt good.*

I found a poem!

Use any piece of writing for this activity. Use an essay or copy a page from a novel for your students. Ask your students to find words and arrange them until they have found a poem.

# Writing Activity 22 — Collecting Poems!

> The aims of this activity are to build poetry-writing and storytelling skills.

Talk to your students about the things they like to collect and make a list of the things they mention. For example:

- Baseball cards
- Movie star photos
- Stuffed animals
- Marbles

Now ask them to each choose one to write a silly poem about.

Maybe it will be about an old lady who collected so many cats that they wouldn't fit in her house anymore. Or what about a girl who collected rare stamps and found out one day that she was rich?

I once read a newspaper article about a retired schoolteacher who collected stamps. He took a whole bag to a stamp dealer, thinking they were worthless. But one turned out to be a very rare stamp worth $11,000! How would you feel if this happened to you? What if someone had just given you that stamp? What would you do?

- "Marcus P. Pringle" by Margriet Ruurs, from *Virtual Maniac*

- "The Pancake Collector" by Jack Prelutsky, from *For Laughing Out Loud*

# Writing Activity 23 —Poetry Places

> The aim of this activity is to practice
> poetry techniques, such as alliteration.

Let's write a poem with a strong sense of setting. Setting is an important part of writing. It will help to *show* the background of a poem or story. Whether a poem is set in the Arctic or in Africa will give it a very different flavor. A poem from the southern United States will make reference to specific sights and customs from that place. The writer might describe objects, places, food, and clothing typical for the area. First, let's read some poetry about places:

- *The Colours of British Columbia* by David Bouchard

- *If You're Not From the Prairie...* by David Bouchard

You can use poetry or picture books with a strong sense of place as examples to create your own version. Use published books as a guideline to encourage students to write about their own environment.

Based on the book, *The Colours of British Columbia*, students of Hillcrest Elementary School in Surrey, British Columbia wrote their own hardcover book. Each primary class buddied up with intermediate students to write poetry. One verse is about a color in the world, the next verse is about that color as seen at the school:

> *We first think of snow,*
> *when white is said,*
> *for kids that's*
> *not a surprise –*
> *We remember the first time*
> *we walked through the doors*
> *and found*
> *Some wonderful finds*
> *The books and the teachers,*
> *eager to paint*
> *magnificent murals*
> *on our canvas-white minds.*

*The Colours of British Columbia*'s illustrator, Michael Tickner, then visited the school and did a presentation on his art, followed by a workshop with students to produce murals in the school and illustrations for the school's version of the book.

Another poem with a strong sense of place is "Where I'm From" by author and teacher George Ella Lyon:

# Where I'm From

*I am from clothespins,*
*from Clorox and carbon-tetrachloride.*
*I am from the dirt under the back porch.*
*(Black, glistening,*
*it tasted like beets.)*
*I am from the forsythia bush*
*the Dutch elm*
*whose long-gone limbs I remember*
*as if they were my own.*

*I'm from fudge and eyeglasses,*
*from Imogene and Alafair.*
*I'm from the know-it-alls*
*and the pass-it-ons,*
*from Perk up! and Pipe down!*
*I'm from He restoreth my soul*
*with a cottonball lamb*
*and ten verses I can say myself.*

*I'm from Artemus and Billie's Branch,*
*fried corn and strong coffee.*
*From the finger my grandfather lost*
*to the auger,*
*the eye my father shut to keep his sight.*

*Under my bed was a dress box*
*spilling old pictures,*
*a sift of lost faces*
*to drift beneath my dreams.*
*I am from those moments—*
*snapped before I budded—*
*leaf-fall from the family tree.*

Mrs. Lyon says: "Besides being a poem in its own right, 'Where I'm From' can be a map for a lot of other writing journeys." Let it guide you into writing poems with your students about the places, the events, and the things that make you up.

I used her advice in a writing workshop. One of the students, Rhiannon, was in fifth grade when she wrote her own version of "Where I'm From":

## Where I'm From

*I am from where fresh water meets the land*
*Where the mountains so mighty touch pure sky*

*I am from a sturdy willow tree*
*And cold, frozen lake water*
*And winds that are barely ever a breeze*

*I am from words of kindness*
*Love with every phrase*
*I stand for what my heart thinks true*

*I am from a place of great literature*
*No good book escaping my grasp*
*Inkheart, Holes, these are the books that I read*

*I am from my mom's lasagna and hamburger soup*
*From "Not today, Ray" and "Are you ready, Sky King?"*
*I am from diaper cream dog to "just think about balloons"*

*I am from nurturing friends and family*
*I am from the memories I store in the words that I write*
*To treasure forever on paper*

Third grader Beverly lives in a very different setting: Singapore. She wrote:

## Where I'm From

*I am from breathtaking mountains,*
*From dim sum and warm crabcakes.*
*I am from sunscreen on my hot face*
*And the warm air of a bustling city.*

For more ideas and to listen to the original poem in the author's voice, visit George Ella Lyon's website: **http://www.georgeellalyon.com/ where.html**.

Writing about the place a student lives, or has visited, can also function as a diary. Esther, age twelve, visited Tofino, British Columbia and wrote this poem:

## A Night in Tofino

*The crest of the moon,*
*The shape of a c,*
*Shining down on Tofino*
*On a foggy night.*

*So many nocturnal*
*Creatures busy at work;*
*Scuttling, jumping,*
*Digging holes in the sand.*

*So few diurnal animals awake,*
*All mostly sleeping quietly*
*In their nest, burrows, and*
*Dense thickets.*

*The waves crash loudly*
*Against the shore*
*Like a small, enjoyable*
*Thunderstorm.*

*Silently, a cougar waits to pounce,*
*The sun slowly makes its way up,*
*Until it hits the horizon*
*Giving a warm glow of satisfaction.*

*All of Tofino if brightened*
*With a new light of blue, red and gold,*
*The stars quickly disappear,*
*And a new day has come.*

There are many options for writing place poems with your students. For example:

- Illustrate them with photos to make a collage of places visited during holidays or studied during social studies.
- Ask your students to write a short poem about their own hometown. They can use alliteration, make a tongue twister, or write a rhyming story.
- Discuss unusual place names. Take out an atlas or map of your county, state, province, or country. Make a list of names of cities, lakes, mountains, etc., that appeal to you. Here are some that I have found by looking at a map:
  - Quake Lake
  - Ulala
  - Idabel
  - Parotee Point
  - Blue Mud Bay
  - Chocolate Lake

These names will sound wonderful in a poem. Suggest to your students that they use these (and their own) to write a poem!

For other examples of funny place names in poems, read:

- "In Kamloops I'll Eat Your Boots" by Dennis Lee , from *Alligator Pie*
- "Kahshe or Chicoutimi" by Dennis Lee, from *Alligator Pie*
- "Kleena Kleene" by Margriet Ruurs, from *Virtual Maniac*
- *Ride a Purple Pelican* by Jack Prelutsky
- "Tongue Twister" by Dennis Lee , from *Alligator Pie*
- *Got Geography* by Lee Bennett Hopkins

One of my favorite picture books is written by Jo Ellen Bogart and illustrated by Barbara Reid: *Gifts*. It is the story of a grandmother who travels the world while sending back gifts for her grandchild. She sends from Africa "a roar of a jungle king" and "a boomerang you can fling'" from Australia. Follow the rhythmic story around the world with your students while tracking it on a map and making a list of items.

## Writing Activity 24 – Name Game

> The aim of this activity is to engage students' imaginations.

Use the phone book to find unusual names of people. Here are some I found in my local phone book:

- Mr. Smart (a teacher)
- Mr. Book (a writer)
- Dr. Pilh
- Bear
- Wilma Wigglesworth

Write a poem about a character using an unusual name. Alliteration often works well in making up fictional names. Ask students to make up a list of fictional names. I think that "Seymour" would be a great name for an eye doctor. How about "Myrtle Mayhem"— what kind of person would she be?

## Writing Activity 25 — Shape Poetry

> The aim of this activity is to play with language.

Shape poems are shaped to represent their topic. Students can have fun shaping their words to show a soccer ball or an ice cream cone when writing about these objects.

First, let's look at samples of shape poetry:

- "The Baker" by Arnold Adolf (this poem is shaped like a pizza), from the book *What's on the Menu?*

- "Play Ball" by Loris Lesynski, from *Nothing Beats A Pizza*

- "First Jump" by Avis Harley, from her book *Fly With Poetry*

Here is my poem about a sailboat:

# S is for Shape!

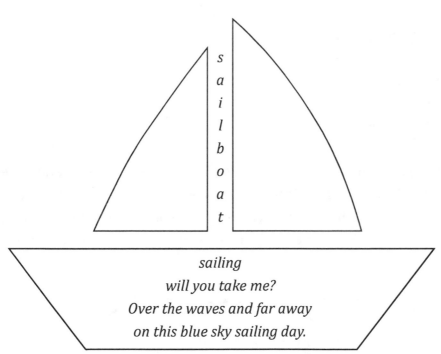

*sailing*
*will you take me?*
*Over the waves and far away*
*on this blue sky sailing day.*

After sharing several shape poems, invite students to create their own. Point out that most shapes are simple lines without details. Help them to think of objects with plain shapes.

Write a "normal" poem first, and then form the sentences into the shape, either using the word processor or hand-write it into a shape. Encourage students to start off with a simple shape. They might try to write about:

- a snake
- an ice cream cone
- a cat
- a flower
- a house
- a piece of pie

How about a heart-shaped Valentine poem or a poem shaped like a Christmas tree? As students get more experienced, try harder shapes. Display their poems around the classroom.

# Writing Activity 26 — High-interest Poems

> The aim of this activity is to make poetry writing relevant to students.

Topics that interest your students can make poetry writing relevant. What is it that your students are interested in? Is there a fad game right now? Which book is everybody reading? Is there a good movie that they've all seen?

Find out what gets your students excited. If you have seventh grade boys, chances are they'll say, "video games!" Try using such a topic in your writing.

Television and video games can give you all sorts of ideas for poems and stories. Invite students to brainstorm ideas from things they've heard about on TV. Let them write a list and then see which of the ideas is suitable to write a poem about.

This discussion might give you an opportunity to discuss the level of violence in some games. How do your students feel about it? What else could make a game exciting to play?

You can use this topic to talk about how much television your students watch and how much time they spend playing video games. Do they feel that it has an effect on them? If so, how? Talk about the positive and negative effects of watching TV and playing certain kinds of games.

What if . . . ? Ask students to write about the kind of game they would create if they worked for a company that designed non-violent video games. Ask them to describe all the details, like the main characters, the places they would go, the things they would need to do, what everything looks like, etc. What would the video game be called? What would the object be?

Or, you might also want to talk about the good news on television. What have you learned by watching TV? What happy things were on the news recently?

Ask students to write a poem about a recent event they saw on television. This could be about a new president being elected, about someone being lost, about someone who won the lottery, etc.

# Writing Activity 27 — Memorizing a Poem

> The aim of this activity is to practice memorization skills.

Memorizing a poem benefits students in many ways. A poem learned in childhood will stay with them for years to come. We often don't use our brains to their full capacity; learning lines from memory activates our brains. Once you have memorized a poem, it can be used for public speaking. Many schools engage in speech art festivals or contests–encourage your students to use poetry to perform at such events.

Ask your students to choose their very favorite poems. These can be poems that they have written themselves or poems by different authors. If a poem by another author is selected, be sure credit is given when reciting it. Start with short poems. I often use my very short poem titled "Phone Poem" (from *Virtual Maniac*) to encourage young students to memorize a poem:

## Phone Poem

*Hello?*
*Oh hi!*
*I know!*
*Gotta go,*
*Goodbye!*

Use hand gestures to pick up a phone when the poem starts, put down the phone when it ends.

Gradually introduce longer poems and encourage students to learn the lines by heart. Let them recite whenever they want to practice. A good book with fun poems to share out loud is *I Did It Because, How A Poem Happens*, by Loris Lesynski and Michael Martchenko.

Recite memorized poems during class time or spread the joy of poetry by sharing at a school assembly or parents' day. Be sure that you, the teacher, memorize and recite a poem, too! Why not use the occasion to memorize a special poem by previous student, your own favorite childhood poem, or one that you wrote yourself?

# Writing Activity 28 — Seasonal Poetry

> The aim of this activity is to build poetry-writing skills by using themes as sources of inspiration.

Use the seasons as a theme to bring poetry into your class. The following books have poems related to seasons or weather. Display these and other books in your classroom. Share them with your students throughout the day.

- *A Circle of Seasons* by Myra Cohn Livingston
- "I Do Not Mind You, Winter Wind" by Jack Prelutsky, from *More Surprises*
- *In for Winter, Out for Spring,* by Arnold Adoff
- *July is a Mad Mosquito* by J. Patrick Lewis
- *Make Things Fly: Poems about the Wind*
- "No," by William Cole, from *More Surprises*
- *Poetry for Young People* by Robert Frost, edited by Gary D. Schmidt
- "A Season," by Lillian M. Fisher, from *More Surprises*
- "Signs of Seasons" by Anonymous, from *More Surprises*
- *Sky Words* by Marilyn Singer
- *Snow, Snow: Winter Poems for Children* by Jane Yolen
- *Under the Cherry Tree* by Satomi Ichikawa and Cynthia Mitchell
- *Voices on the Wind: Poems for all Seasons* selected by David Booth
- *A Winter's Yarn* by Kathleen Cook Waldron
- "Winter Weather" by Margriet Ruurs from *Virtual Maniac*

After reading a wide variety of both humorous and serious poems about the time of year, follow up by inviting your students to write about their favorite seasons.

Seasonal celebrations such as Christmas or Hanukkah can also be used to inspire poetry. Read published poems and use each celebration to create

your own classroom poems. Here are some examples to share
with your students:

## GENERAL CELEBRATIONS
- *Celebrations* by Myra Cohn Livingston
- "A Circle of Seasons" by Myra Cohn Livingston
- *Festivals* by Myra Cohn Livingston

## HALLOWEEN
- *Best Witches: Poems for Halloween* by Jane Yolen
- *Catmagic* by Loris Lesynski
- "Mother Goblin's Lullaby" by Jack Prelutsky, from *Something Big Has Been Here*
- *Halloween Poems* by Myra Cohn Livingston
- *Halloween Stories & Poems* by Carolyn Feller Bauer
- *Scared Silly! A Book for the Brave* by Marc Brown
- *Teachers' Night Before Halloween* by Steven Layne
- "Whose Boo Is Whose?" by X. J. Kennedy, from *For Laughing Out Loud*
- "Witch Goes Shopping" by Lilian Moore, from *For Laughing Out Loud*

## CHRISTMAS
- *Christmas Poems* by Myra Cohn Livingston
- *The Night Before Christmas* by Clement Clarke Moore
- *The Principal's Night Before Christmas* by Steven Layne
- *Silent Night: The Song From Heaven* by Linda Granfield
- *Teacher's Night Before Christmas* by Steven Layne

## VALENTINE'S DAY
- *Good morning to you, Valentine: Poems* by Lee Bennett Hopkins
- *Valentine's Day: Stories and Poems* edited by Carolyn Feller Bauer

Valentine poems, of course, are traditional. You can send home students' own poems as Valentine cards.

But you can also use humor to give poems your own twist. That is what Ashley (age fourteen) did when she wrote this poem:

### February 15

*It's the day after Valentine's Day,*
*The roses have wilted*
*The card is in the trash,*
*The chocolates he gave me*
*Made me fat.*
*Valentine's Day*
*So much for that.*

*I wanted*
*A candlelight dinner*
*Or a diamond ring*
*But instead he broke up with me.*
*Valentine's Day.*
*So much for that.*

## Writing Activity 29 — Whose Viewpoint?

> The aim of this activity is to create awareness of different points of view in writing.

Writing an existing story or poem from a different viewpoint can shed a whole new light on the story line. Look at the following poem:

# School Sick

*I don't want to go to school today.*
*I think I'll be sick so I can stay*
*in my bed, cozy and warm.*
*I don't want to go out in rain and storm.*
*I'll throw up all over the rug*
*and crawl back to bed, comfy 'n snug.*

*I'll fake a sore throat*
*and a fever.*
*My mom is smart*
*but I can deceive her!*
*I'll have funny lumps with a rash*
*so she'll want me back in bed in a flash.*
*That way I can stay home and play,*
*slumber and snooze the entire day.*

*Uh oh*
*Here comes my mom with bottles and a pill,*
*she takes my temperature, I have to lie very still!*
*I don't want to swallow that*
*I just may have to get out of bed!*
*The medicine has a terrible smell,*
*And all of a sudden I feel very well!*

(Margriet Ruurs, *Virtual Maniac*)

Ask your students: "Whose viewpoint are we hearing? How would the story line be different if we heard the same thing from the mother's point of view? Here is what I think the mother would say:

> *Oh no, not another day!*
> *What if he wants to stay*
> *in bed, at home, with me...*
> *How could I watch TV*
> *Or eat my secret chocolate stash?*
> *He doesn't really have a rash!*
> *I have to think and fast!*
> *I'll give him a true-sickness test.*
> *Some Buckley's in his cream of wheat*
> *Should put him right back on his feet.*
> *I know my boy is kind of cool*
> *But I just want him back in school!*

Challenge students to write this story from a teacher's point of view or a friend's. Who else could we use? Is there perhaps a mouse under the bed, listening in? Is there a little sister? What about writing the story from the medicine bottle's point of view?

Try rewriting a poem from a different viewpoint with a variety of poems, such as:

- "My Dog Is Too Friendly" by Bruce Lansky, from *Poetry Party.* Can you write it from the dog's point of view?

- "The Black Bear" by Jack Prelutsky, from *Bear in Mind: A Book of Bear Poems.* Can you write it from the bear's point of view?

# Writing Activity 30 — Adding Rhyme to Reason

> The aim of this activity is to make poetry a cross-curricular skill.

Add some spice to math lessons by sprinkling in some poetry. You can rap multiplication tables. Instead of just saying them, rap them. Clap the tune or stamp your feet and fall into a rap rhythm:

*Ten - times - four*
*Ten - ten - ten - times - four - four - four is*
*pff-ahh-pff-ahh-ahh*
*for-ty - for-ty*

Use poetry books with a math theme like the ones below. Read them with your students, and let them inspire you to write your own math poems. Your students could write about selling a toy and what they would do with the money, or they can write a poem about saving pennies and counting them. How about a poem in which they count books in the library? In Sheree Fitch's book, *Sleeping Dragons All Around,* you will encounter Pythagorus, the mathematical dragon. Use him as an example of writing math poetry.

These books and poems will help you on the way to adding rhythm to math.

- *Adventures of Penrose the Mathematical Cat* by Theoni Pappas
- *Animal Hours* by Linda Manning
- *Fractals, Googols, and Other Mathematical Tales* by Theoni Pappas
- *Grapes of Math* by Greg Tang
- *If You Made a Million* by David M. Schwartz (This book does not rhyme but is lots of fun to use in math and adapts easily for students to write their own "Million" poems.)

- *Math Talk: Mathematical Ideas in Poems for Two Voices* by Theoni Pappas
- "The Monkey" and "Allison Beals and Her 25 Eels" by Shel Silverstein, from *Falling Up*
- "I Pulled An 'A' in Math" by Gordon Korman and Bernice Korman, from *The D- Poems of Jeremy Bloom*
- *A Remainder of One* by Elinor J. Pinczes
- *Mathematickles!* by Betsy Franco
- *Marvelous Math: A Book of Poems* by Lee Bennett Hopkins (Aladdin Picture Books)

For a plethora of math poems, check out this teaching resource: *Math Poetry, Linking Language and Math in a Fresh Way* by Betsy Franco.

# Writing Activity 31 — Take One Line and Add Words

> The aim of this activity is to build poetry-writing skills by using accompanying works as inspiration.

Use published books to inspire students' poems. In the school library, find a collection of picture books that have very little text. Some suggested books include:

- *The Happy Day* by Marc Simont
- *Jessie's Island* by Sheryl McFarlane
- *A Mountain Alphabet* by Margriet Ruurs
- *A Prairie Alphabet* by Jo Bannatyne-Cugnet
- *When the Wind Stops* by Charlotte Zolotow

Ask your students to select one of the books, read through the different pages, and then choose one line. That line becomes the first sentence of their poem.

For instance, in *A Mountain Alphabet* I used this sentence for the letter "R": *Rambunctious raccoons can be real rascals.* If a student chooses this line, his or her poem might look like the following:

## Raccoons

*Rambunctious raccoons can be real rascals*
*The little bandits give me a fright*
*as they clatter in garbage cans*
*in the dark alley at the night.*

You can also use picture books without any text. Students can select an image and write a story or poem to accompany it. Check out these wordless picture books that can inspire students to do their own writing:

- *Sunshine* by Jan Ormerod
- *The Window* by Jeannie Baker
- *Zoom* by Istvan Banyai

# Writing Activity 32 — Personification

> The aim of this activity is to create awareness of personification as a poetry-writing technique.

Explain to your students that "personification" means that we turn an animal or an object into a person by letting them do things that only people can really do. For instance, a bee that is thinking or a house that is waiting. Personification is great to use in poems because it allows us to make a bear laugh or a flower dance. Wordstorm personification possibilities with your students. What kind of traits or actions can they attribute to an animal or an object?

Use these books and poems as examples:

- *There's a Mouse in My House* by Sheree Fitch

- "The Dodo," by Peter Wesley-Smith, from *For Laughing Out Loud*

As an example, you can share this poem by Avis Harley from her book *Fly With Poetry*:

## Editing the Chrysalis

*"At Last," cried Butterfly,*
*Poised*
*Over its*
*Empty chrysalis,*
*"My final draft!"*

Discuss the poem with your students: A butterfly doesn't speak. It doesn't write a final draft. But in poetry, it can. Did you notice that this poem is also an acrostic? We will revisit this poem for Writing Activity 34 when we discuss acrostics.

Invite your students to write a personification poem about their favorite animal or object.

# The Flower

*Have you seen the glory of a flower*
*that stands proudly over the pond*
*Staring all day long*
*at its own reflection?*

*Have you seen the way*
*she holds her head in triumph*
*looking down upon the grass*
*at how small the blades are*
*in her shadow?*

*Have you seen the vainness*
*in a flower that reflects*
*in the still waters*
*that ripple slightly*
*and then shatter*
*the flower's image?*

(Ashley, grade 9)

# Writing Activity 33 — Reflective Poetry

> The aim of this activity is to teach students to take information about themselves and turn it into a poem.

In the poem "Abandoned Farmhouse" by Ted Kooser, past Poet Laureate of the United States, we learn about a man long-gone. We see glimpses of his past through objects left behind. The entire poem can be found on the The Poetry Out Loud webpage, presented by the National Endowment for the Arts and The Poetry Foundation: **http://www.poetryoutloud.org/poems/poem.html?id=237648**.

Using the first verse of this poem, students can create their own poetry while reflecting on what makes them unique. Which objects in your house or room can give us information about the kind of person you are?

Start by asking students to close their eyes and picture the scene in their minds as you read, slowly, aloud:

# Abandoned Farmhouse

*He was a big man, says the size of his shoes*
*on a pile of broken dishes by the house;*
*a tall man too, says the length of the bed*
*in an upstairs room; and a good, God-fearing man,*
*says the Bible with a broken back*
*on the floor below the window, dusty with sun;*
*but not a man for farming, say the fields*
*cluttered with boulders and the leaky barn.*

After listening to the verse, ask students to describe the picture this poem painted in their minds. Discuss the information, making a point of asking students "who or what gave us the information about this person whom we have never met?" Examples include:

- It was the shoes and the bed that told us the size of the man
- It was the Bible that showed us he read it a lot. How do we know that he read it often? What does a book look like if you read it over and over?
- Point out the fact that the voice is in the third person and that it speaks in the past tense: "he *was...*"

Next, make a list on the blackboard of the information we received including the "but" at the end with the statement that he was not a good farmer. When doing this activity with students, I write down:

1.  He was big (told by the shoes)
2.  He was tall (told by the bed)
3.  He read a lot (told by a tattered Bible)

BUT . . .
4. He was not a good farmer (told by the boulders and a leaking barn).

Now, invite students to make their own list of three pieces of information about themselves, followed by a "but. . ."—something they are not good at or don't like to do.

Nick, in sixth grade, made a list that included:

1.  Likes to play video games (high score)
2.  Plays soccer (ball)
3.  Likes pizza (empty boxes)

BUT
4. Is not good at math (mark)

He decided on the objects that would convey the information in his poem as well as on just the right adjectives. Nick's poem now reads:

> *He was excelled at playing video games*
> *says the unbeatable high score,*
> *He loved soccer,*
> *says the scruffy ball;*
> *He sure liked pizza,*
> *say the empty boxes on the kitchen table*
> *But he wasn't very good at math,*
> *says the C on his report card.*

When you guide your students into writing this poetry format, be sure to write a similar poem about yourself, to share with your class. They may be surprised to learn that you like knitting or have a cat at home. Poems can be illustrated and displayed as biographical pieces.

# Writing Activity 34—Puzzle Poems

> The aim of this activity is to practice the acrostic poetry format.

Acrostics are fun because they are word puzzles that can make writing poetry an exciting activity. When I first model writing an acrostic to a group of students, I don't tell them what we are going to do. I tell them that we will now write a fun poem about . . . their teacher! Knowing that the teacher's name is, for instance, Ms. Brown, I invite students to give me information about her. I ask questions such as:

- What is she like?
- What does she enjoy doing?
- What is her favorite subject to teach?
- Does she have a family, like dogs, loves swimming?

I make notes on the board before writing sentences, writing down their answers: she is nice, she likes to read, she likes animals, she is interesting, etc. Once I have sufficient information, I start on my poem:

*My teacher is really nice.*
*She loves to read*
*Books about animals,*
*Reads poems*
*Or novels. Anything!*
*Wonderful teacher,*
*Never boring*

I show students how this poem has short sentence but doesn't rhyme. We read it several times, perhaps do some editing. Then I tell them that the best part about this poem is that it has a secret message hidden in it. Who can spot the secret message? Someone is bound to discover that the first letters of each line spell her name: Ms. Brown.

You can model this in the same way, using your own name or the name of the school principal or librarian. You can also use a book character, asking students for information about this character. Without pointing it out, use the first letters to spell the name.

Now invite students to think of information to share about themselves: favorite subjects in school, sports, food, animals. Ask students to write short sentences about themselves, using the first letters of each line to spell their own name.

In Writing Activity 32, we read a poem by Avis Harley called "Editing The Chrysalis." Use this poem now to show your students the surprise message. This poem is an acrostic and spells "A POEM" when the first letters of each word are read vertically. I particularly like Avis Harley's triple acrostic titled, "A Rock Acrostic."

**A Rock Acrostic:**

| Inside | these | deep |
|---|---|---|
| tunnels | of rock | echo |
| soft | rhythms like | the |
| faint beat of | earth's | heart; |
| under this | ancient | layer |
| new stalactites | drip | steadily. |

In this triple acrostic, the first letters of the initial and middle words and the final letters of the last words have a meaning when read downward. As this sample poem demonstrates, the sky is the limit when creating acrostics. Students can write an acrostic poem about any topic they are studying: a book report can be written as an acrostic using the book's title.

You can write an acrostic about animals, planets, transportation, countries, and more. Simply decide on the general topic and have students select their own specific subject for a poem. On a sheet of paper, each student can make a list of information about their word. Next, print each letter of the word in a vertical line and fill in the blanks.

My general topic of a sample poem will be "countries." More specifically, I chose the country "Mongolia" since I recently visited it. My list of information about Mongolia will include:

| | |
|---|---|
| camels | cold |
| gers (yurts) | mountains |
| horses | smiles |
| cheese | herds |
| open spaces | tundra |
| sky | Genghis Khan |
| friendly | people |
| music | |
| trains | |

I now spell the word from top to bottom and fill in the blanks with either one word or a sentence. My acrostic poem can—but doesn't have to—rhyme.

M iles and miles of
O open spaces,
N omads living in solitude
G oats, camels, horses grazing
O n endless tundra.
L aughter of many smiling faces,
I feel privileged to be here,
A mazing land of Genghis Khan.

In this sample poem, I used sentences. I can also write an acrostic as a list poem by simply listing words that spell the topic:

T  ireless hunter
I   n Africa
G  rowling
E  nemy
R  oaming the jungle.

After your students create their own acrostics, they can share them without revealing the title. Can others guess which word their poem spells out?

# Writing Activity 35 — Diamante Poems

> The aim of this activity is to practice the diamante poetry format.

Writing a diamante poem uses skills that are helpful throughout the writing process since it helps students to focus on descriptive words and antonyms. A diamante poem progresses from one concept in the first line to its opposite in the last line.

This diamond-shaped poem is seven lines long, centered on the page. The traditional form contains antonyms in Lines 1 and 7 and descriptive words about these nouns. The forms is as follows:

Line 1  One noun, an antonym or contrast to Line 7
Line 2  Two adjectives that describe Line 1
Line 3  Three gerunds (verbs with -ing endings) that
          relate to the word in Line 1
Line 4  Four nouns, the first two relate to Line 1,
          the second two relate to Line 7
Line 5  Three gerunds that relate to Line 7

Line 6  Two adjectives that describe the word in Line 7
Line 7  One noun, an antonym or contrast to Line 1

Thirteen-year-old Jack wrote a diamante poem about his favorite sports:

*Soccer*
*speed, ability*
*kicking, blocking, running*
*field, ball, puck, ice*
*checking, shooting, skating*
*agility, skill*
*Hockey*

Use diamante poems to analyze characters in novels you read with your students. I recently read the novel *I, Coriander* by Sally Gardner. I created this diamante poem about two of the main characters, Coriander and Hester:

*Coriander*
*courageous, magical*
*promising, exciting, loving*
*gentle, lonely, beaten, defeated*
*trusting, believing, ailing*
*hopeful, expectant*
*Hester*

Creating a diamante poem about fictional characters helps students to realize how opposite characters work to create story. It also helps to determine more clearly the traits of a main character.

Write diamante poems when discussing a novel, when studying social studies (continents, countries, trades), or even to connect writing to science topics such as animals, the environment, or seasons.

Not only will this exercise help your students to define characters in existing books or in their own writing, but it opens the mind to a wealth of adjectives and helps relate poems to the reading and writing your class is involved in.

A good classroom resource is *Teach Writing to Older Readers Using Picture Books: Every Picture Tells a Story*, by Jane Heitman.

For examples, guidelines and even a template, check out PIZZAZ (People Interested in Zippy and ZAny Zcribbling), an online resource for scribblers and teachers of English to speakers of other languages (ESOL): **http://www.uoregon.edu/~leslieob/diamantes.html**.

The Online Learning Studio is a teacher-created website full of reading and writing activities. It helps students create their own diamante poems step by step: **http://www.boobis.com/students/poetry/diamante.html**.

# Writing Activity 36—Shadow or Loop Poetry

> The aim of this activity is to inspire poetry through wordplay.

Here's another fun way to have students "whip up" a poem. Reuse the last word of each line as the first word in the next line:

*A dog has four legs,*
*Legs for running,*
*Running to chase a cat.*
*Cat, not this dog's best friend.*

Randi is in grade 9 and wrote a loop poem using a slightly different format: she used the first word twice before using the last word in the second line as her first word in the next line:

## Eyes that Love

*Apple of the tree*
*Apple of my eye*
*Eyes that see*
*Eyes are blind*
*Blind men grope*
*Blind will see*
*See the hope*
*See the light*
*Light that dims*
*Light that shines*
*Shines with glory*
*Shines so bright*
*Bright lights*
*Bright nights*
*Nights are long*
*Nights are dark*
*Dark is alone*
*Dark is overcome*
*Overcome with love*
*Overcome with faith*
*Faith conquers*
*Faith believes*
*Believes in mercy*
*Believes in forgiving*
*Forgiving mistakes*
*Forgiving our past*
*Past that haunts*
*Past that lives*
*Lives in us*

*Lives with fear*
*Fear of ourselves*
*Fear that sticks*
*Sticks in our mind*
*Sticks in our life*
*Life of disappointment*
*Life of regret*
*Regrets are forgiven*
*Regret is behind*
*Behind our troubles*
*Behind our pain*
*Pain of yesterday*
*Pain is healed*
*Healed forever*
*Healed hearts*
*Hearts are saved*
*Hearts that love*
*Love that cares*
*Love unconditionally*
*Unconditionally*
*Cares.*

Challenge your students to write poems in a similar way—and have fun playing with language!

# Writing Activity 37 — Poems by Definition*

> The aim of this activity is to use vocabulary
> to inspire poetry.

Poems, by definition, are small packages of words giving its own unique view on a topic. Poet Sara Holbrook developed a fun format to use poetry-writing in the classroom by writing "definition poems." As the title implies, you can use this format to define any word. This activity is especially useful with students in middle and high school but can be adapted for any grade level.

1.  Select a word: this can be any word from the week's vocabulary list, from a topic you are studying in science or social studies, a difficult word encountered in a text, or even a title or the name of a character from a book your class is reading. If at all possible, let each student select his or her own word to define.

2.  Ask students to look up the word's meaning in the dictionary (if applicable). They should also search for synonyms. Ms. Holbrook says: "a word is not only defined by what it is, but also by what it is not."

3.  Next, fold a regular sheet of paper in half width-wise.

| On the left side, write: | On the right side, write: |
|---|---|
| is - | is not - |
| can - | cannot - |
| positives - | negatives - |
| synonyms (another word for) - | antonyms (opposite meaning) - |

4.  Fill in the blanks. What "is" it? What can it do? What is good about it? What else can you call it?

On the right side, list opposites to your word. What is it not? What can it *not* do or accomplish, and so forth. As the teacher, be sure to try this exercise yourself with a word of your own choosing.

I recently visited Manila in the Philippines, and so chose that city as the topic for my sample definition poem.

SAMPLE: Manila

**is** - a busy city, many buildings, roads, tuk-tuks, a fun place to visit
**can** - make me feel small, insignificant
**positives** - friendly people, interesting sites, old buidings, culture
**synonyms** - capital of the Philippines, urban, metropolis

**is not** - where I'd like to live, a small town
**cannot** - be quiet, be small
**negatives** - I get lost, don't speak local language
**antonyms** - rainforest, oasis

Now, using some of the "definitions" of Manila, I write my poem:

## Manila

*Bustling city, not an oasis but*
*a labyrinth of roads*
*choking with tuk-tuks and taxis,*
*a metropolis of cell phones*
*and flashing neon signs.*
*Not a quiet country lane*
*where I can hear crickets chirp.*
*Its broad avenues lined*
*with lipstick palms*
*and smiling vendors*
*"Yes, m'am, no m'am!"*
*Manila -*
*cannot be defined.*

Note that I did not use all words in my final poem. I selected some and listened for rhythm when I edited the poem, adding a new adjective or finding a new image that worked.

Paul is in fifth grade and wrote the definition of a poem but chose to write it in the first person:

## A Poem

*I am a short meaningful story*
*and invoke feelings*
*as I flow off the tongue like water.*
*I am a rhythmic tale and not*
*a clumsily worded book.*

*I cannot and will never be*
*a mixture of thoughtless words.*
*I won't be a picture, but I'll*
*make one in your head.*

*Used with permission from Practical Poetry (Heinemann 2005) and High Definition (Heinemann 2010) by Sara Holbrook and Michael Salinger. More inspiring poems and information can be found on Sara Holbrook's website: **www.saraholbrook.com**.

# Chapter 3: Bibliography and Websites

## BIBLIOGRAPHY

Adoff, Arnold, and Jerry Pinkney. *In for Winter, Out for Spring.* New York: Harcourt, 1997.

Bagert, Brod. *Let Me Be the Boss: Poems for Kids to Perform.* Honesdale, Penn.: Boyds Mills Press, 1992.

Baker, Jeannie. *The Window.* Walker Books, 2002.

Bannatyne-Cugnet, Jo. *A Prairie Alphabet.* Toronto: Tundra Books, 2009.

Base, Graeme. *The Eleventh Hour.* Don Mills, Ont.: Stoddart Publishing, 1988.

Base, Graeme. *The Sign of the Seahorse: A Tale of Greed and High Adventure in Two Acts.* New York: Harry N. Abrams, 1992.

Bauer, Carolyn Feller. *Halloween: Stories & Poems.* New York: HarperCollins, 1992.

Bauer, Carolyn Feller. *Valentine's Day: Stories and Poems.* New York: HarperCollins, 1993.

Banyai, Istvan. *Zoom.* Puffin, 1998.

Booth, David. *Voices on the Wind: Poems for all Seasons.* William Morrow & Co, 1990.

Brett, Jan. *The Mitten.* New York: G. P. Putnam & Sons, 1989.

Brown, Marc. *Scared Silly! A Book for the Brave.* Boston: Little Brown and Co., 1994.

Bogart, Jo Ellen. *Gifts.* Scholastic, 1996.

Burleigh, Robert. *Hoops.* San Diego: Harcourt Brace, 1997.

Carroll, Lewis. *Jabberwocky.* Boston: Harry N.Abrams, 1989.

Cole, Joanna and Stephanie Calmensen. *Six Sick Sheep: 101 Tongue Twisters*

Conford, Ellen. *A Royal Pain.* New York: Scholastic, 1986.

Day, David, and Aska Warabé. *Aska's Animals.* Toronto: Doubleday Canada, 1991.

Feelings, Tom. *Soul Looks Back in Wonder.* New York: Dial Books, 1993.

Fitch, Sheree. *Sleeping Dragons All Around.* Toronto: Doubleday Canada, 1989.

Fitch, Sheree. *There's a Mouse in My House.* Toronto: Doubleday Canada, 1997.

Fitch, Sheree. *Toes in My Nose: And Other Poems.* Toronto: Doubleday Canada, 1987.

Franco, Betsy. *Mathematickles*, McElderry, 2006.

Frost, Robert. *Poetry for Young People*, edited by Gary D. Schmidt

Goldstein, Bobbye S. *Bear in Mind: A Book of Bear Poems.* New York: Viking Kestrel, 1989.

Goldstein, Bobbye S. *What's on the Menu?* New York: Viking Juvenile, 1992.

Granfield, Linda. *Silent Night: The Song From Heaven.* Tundra, 2000.

Harley, Avis. *Fly with Poetry: An ABC of Poetry.* Honesdale, Penn.: Boyds Mill Press, 2000.

Heitman, Jane. *Teach Writing to Older Readers Using Picture Books: Every Picture Tells a Story*. Linworth, 2005.

Holbrook, Sara and and Michael Salinger. *Practical Poetry*. Heinemann 2005

Holbrook, Sara and and Michael Salinger, *High Definition*. Heinemann 2010.

Hopkins, Lee Bennett. *Dinosaurs.* Orlando: Harcourt Brace, 1987.

Hopkins, Lee Bennett. *More Surprises* (an "I Can Read Book"). New York: Harper & Row, 1987.

Hopkins, Lee Bennett. *Good Morning to You, Valentine: Poems for Valentine's Day*. HBJ, 1976

Hopkins, Lee Bennett. *Marvelous Math: A Book of Poems*, Simon & Schuster, 2001.

Hopkins, Lee Bennett. *Spectacular Science: A Book of Poems* . Simon & Schuster, 2002.

Hopkins, Lee Bennett. *Got Geography*. Greenwillow Books, 2006.

Hyman, Trina Schart. *Little Red Riding Hood.* New York: Holiday House, 1987.

Ichikawa, Satomi, and Cynthia Mitchell. *Under the Cherry Tree.* New York: William Collins, 1979.

Kellogg, Steven. *Aster Aardvark's Alphabet Adventures.* New York: Morrow Junior Books, 1987.

Kennedy, Dorothy M. *Make Things Fly: Poems about the Wind.* New York: Margaret K. McElderry Books, 1998.

Korman, Gordon, and Bernice Korman. *The D- Poems of Jeremy Bloom: A Collection of Poems About School, Homework, and Life.* New York: Scholastic, 1992.

Lansky, Bruce. *Poetry Party.* New York: Meadowbrook Press, 1996.

Layne, Steven. *The Principal's Night Before Christmas.* Pelican Publishing, 2004.

Layne, Steven. *Teacher's Night Before Christmas.* Pelican Publising, 2001.

Lear, Edward. *The Complete Nonsense of Edward Lear.* New York: Dover Publications, 1951.

Lee, Dennis. *Alligator Pie.* Toronto: Macmillan of Canada, 1974.

Lee, Dennis. *The Ice Cream Store.* New York: HarperCollins, 1991.

Lesynski, Loris. *Catmagic.* Toronto: Annick Press, 1998.

Lesynski, Loris. *Nothing Beats A Pizza.* Annick, 2001.

Lesynski, Loris. *I Did It Because, How A Poem Happens.* Annick, 2006.

Lewis, J. Patrick. *July is a Mad Mosquito.* New York: Atheneum, 1994.

Livingston, Myra Cohn. *Christmas Poems.* New York: Holiday House, 1988.

Livingston, Myra Cohn. *A Circle of Seasons.* New York: Holiday House, 1982.

Livingston, Myra Cohn. *Halloween Poems.* New York: Holiday House, 1989.

Livingston, Myra Cohn. *Festivals.* Holiday House, 1996.

Livingston, Myra Cohn. *Celebration*s. Scholastic, 1991.

Livingston, Myra Cohn. *Poem-Making: Ways to Begin Writing Poetry*. HarperCollins, 1991.

Manning, Linda. *Animal Hours.* Don Mills, Ont.: Oxford University Press, 1990.

McFarlane, Sheryl. *Jessie's Island.* Victoria, B.C.: Orca Books,1992.

Moore, Clement Clarke. *The Night Before Christmas.* Buffalo: Firefly Books, 1999.

Okutoro, Lydia. *Quiet Storm, Voices of Young Black Poets.* New York: Hyperion Books, 1999.

Ormerod, Jan. *Sunshine*. Frances Lincoln Children's Books, 2009.

Pappas, Theoni. *The Adventures of Penrose the Mathematical Cat*. San Carlos, Cali.: Wide World Publishing/Tetra, 1997.

Pappas, Theoni. *Fractals, Googols, and Other Mathematical Tales*. San Carlos, Cali.: Wide World Publishing, 1993.

Pappas, Theoni. *Math Talk: Mathematical Ideas in Poems for Two Voices*. San Carlos, Cali.: Wide World Publishing, 1991.

Paulsen, Gary. *Hatchet*. New York: Puffin Books, 1987.

Pearson, Kit. *Awake and Dreaming*. Toronto: Puffin Books, 1999.

Peet, Bill. *The Whingdingdilly*. Boston: Houghton Mifflin, 1970.

Pinczes, Elinor J. *A Remainder of One*. Boston: Houghton Mifflin, 1995.

Prelutsky, Jack. *For Laughing Out Loud: Poems to Tickle Your Funnybone*. New York: Alfred A. Knopf, 1991.

Prelutsky, Jack. *Ride A Purple Pelican*. New York: Greenwillow Books, 1986.

Prelutsky, Jack. *The Sheriff of Rottenshot*. New York: Greenwillow Books, 1982.

Prelutsky, Jack. *Something Big Has Been Here*. New York: Scholastic, 1992.

Reid, Barbara. *Two by Two*. Toronto: North Winds Press, 1992.

Reid, Barbara. The Party. Scholastic, 1999.

Ruurs, Margriet. *A Mountain Alphabet*. Toronto: Tundra Books, 1996.

Ruurs, Margriet. *Virtual Maniac: Silly and Serious Poems for Kids*. Gainesville, Fla.: Maupin House Publishing, 2000.

Ruurs, Margriet. *Animal Alphabed*. Boyds Mills Press, 2005

Ruurs, Margriet. *A Pacific Alphabet*, Whitecap, 2001

Schwartz, David M. *If You Made a Million*. New York: Mulberry Books, 1989.

Service, Robert. *The Cremation of Sam McGee*. Toronto: Kids Can Press, 2006.

Seuss, Dr. *Yertle the Turtle*. New York: Random House, 1950.

Silverstein, Shel. *Falling Up*. New York: HarperCollins, 1996.

Simont, Marc. *The Happy Day*. New York: Harper & Row, 1980.

Singer, Marilyn. *Sky Words.* New York: Macmillan Publishing, 1994.

Tang, Greg. *The Grapes of Math*. Scholastic, 2004.

Tang, Greg. *Math-terpieces*. Scholastic, 2003.

Vaccaro Seeger, Laura. *What If?* Roaring Brook Press, 2010

Waldron Cook, Kathleen. *A Winter's Yarn*. Red Deer Press, 1986.

Woolger, David. *The Magic Tree.* Toronto: Oxford University Press, 1987.

Yolen, Jane. *Best Witches: Poems for Halloween.* New York: G.P. Putnam's Sons, 1989.

Yolen, Jane. *Owl Moon.* New York: Scholastic, 1987.

Yolen, Jane. *Snow, Snow: Winter Poems for Children.* Honesdale, Penn.: Boyds Mills Press, 1998.

Young, Sue. *The Scholastic Rhyming Dictionary.* New York: Scholastic, 1997.

Zolotow, Charlotte. *When the Wind Stops.* New York: HarperCollins, 1997.


## WEBSITES

To create your own diamante poem online, go to: **http://www.boobis.com/students/poetry/diamante.html**.

Flocabulary ™ brings hip-hop into the classroom by adding rap to various areas of the curriculum. To view examples by subject area, go to: **http://www.flocabulary.com**.

George Ella Lyon's website: **http://www.georgeellalyon.com/where.html**.

For the complete text of the poem "Abandoned Farmhouse" by Ted Kooser, visit the Poetry Out Loud website: **http://www.poetryoutloud.org/poems/poem.html?id=237648**.

For online rhyming dictionaries, visit RhymeZone: **http://www.rhymezone.com** or WriteExpress' Rhymer **http://www.rhymer.com**.

For more poetry writing ideas, go to Sara Holbrook's website: **http://www.saraholbrook.com**.

For instructions and exercises with diamante poems for ESOL teachers, visit the PIZZAZ website: **http://www.uoregon.edu/~leslieob/diamantes.html**.

**CHAPTER 4**

# The Editing Process

Author James Michener said, "I'm not a very good writer, but I'm an excellent rewriter." All writers have to edit and rewrite if they hope to share or publish their writing.

Now that your students have completed writing several different forms of poetry, look back at the sheets full of poems they have collected in their binders. Having fun with words has allowed them to marvel at language and to shape poetry. We now are ready to take that rough piece of wood and do some sanding to make it nice and smooth, to do some editing to make each poem even better.

I would like to make clear what I see as the difference between editing and critiquing. Critiquing should come first and entails taking a critical look at the overall poem: contents, message, general word use. Does it convey the right image? Editing refers more to grammar, punctuation, and sentence structure.

## Critiquing

As students near the completion of a first draft, I make a point of sitting down with each one to critique his or her poem. My main concerns, at this point, are content and mastery of the craft. I ask questions like these:

- Is the writing going the way you wanted it?
- Are you happy with it?
- Does the poem say what you wanted it to say?
- Are your words painting the pictures you see in your head?

Keep in mind that the student should make the decisions that change his or her own writing. All you should do is make (verbal) suggestions and show possible improvement, but the writer should remain in charge of the piece he or she created. Try to guide your students by showing them examples of problems and by making suggestions for change where appropriate. Make suggestions such as:

- How would this sound if . . .
- What if you change this sentence around so you have an easier word to rhyme with?
- Should this be a rhyming poem?

Try to discuss rewriting in a manner that will encourage students rather than overwhelm them. For one student it might be adding a funny ending or finding a different name for a character. Other students can handle more complicated restructuring, such as adding more senses or writing the poem from a different viewpoint.

Although you will want to be kind to each author, it is also important that your students grow from your feedback. Telling a student how wonderful his or her poem is will not help improve their next piece of writing. Try to find several positive points to comment on, but also try to give constructive feedback that will help to improve the student's writing. Concentrate on helping a student to achieve his or her goals. Try not to react personally. Whether you like the contents is not important. Did the student reach his or her goal of touching the reader, of conveying the message? Did the student use his or her knowledge of craft to create the poem?

# Peer Conferencing

Realistically, it is difficult to conference with each student in a class of many! You may want to spread conferencing out over several days or spend a few minutes with each student while the rest of the class is reading. Another way to critique is to team up students and ask them to work together, giving you time to work with individuals. Students can learn to act as effective editors for each other. Discuss criteria beforehand with the entire group. Students reading another student's writing should explain to the writer:

- I liked your poem because . . .
- What I don't like about it is . . .
- You have used alliteration/metaphor/simile and this is what I think about it . . .
- The beat/rhythm works or doesn't work

I strongly suggest that the students read the poem out loud because this allows them to hear which lines have too many syllables and which lines need an extra word. This may include substituting a word of two syllables for one with more or fewer syllables. Reading the poem aloud will help to find the right rhythm. Say to them: "Does the poem have the right beat? Can you hear that one line is too long? Clap along while you say the poem out loud. Find the right rhythm for each line."

The other students in your class can also serve as a source of inspiration. Encourage your students to talk to each other for ideas and suggestions after plenty of conference modeling. Once a student asked me, "What is a good name for a wizard?" I suggested he ask the group for suggestions and then choose the one he liked best. Great ideas poured forth:

- "Look in *The Lord of the Rings*."
- "Spell your own name backwards!"
- "Find a foreign word for wizard," etc.

The suggestions were much more creative than what I would have come up with. Students' suggestions help other students to find new directions for their writing, often giving them renewed energy to write more. But ultimately they are just that—suggestions. The student should be treated as an author in charge of his or her own writing, editing, and rewriting, deciding for him or herself what to add, where to change something, or which advice to disregard.

The feedback might give the writer good ideas for a complete rewriting of the poem. Or, the student might decide to change parts of the poem, shorten a sentence, take out a word, change a line. The writer might also decide that he or she doesn't agree with a particular suggestion and ignore it. Some poems are perfect the first time around. But many do need some "sanding." Once the writer is satisfied with the overall poem, ask him or her to correct spelling (using the spell check function or dictionary). Correcting punctuation can once again be done through peer conferencing.

At this point, students who are not used to having the freedom to choose their own topics often discover that they really do have the power to take their writing in any direction they want. They might ask questions, such as "Can this happen in outer space?" or "Can I make her die at the end?" They delight in the idea that the story line is theirs to take in any direction they choose.

In some cases, kids discover that they were not committed enough to their first idea, that they got bored with it. If that happens, they can look back at their list of ideas and choose a new topic, one with more interesting aspects. Practice makes perfect, right? They thrive with the freedom of choice, even if they now have to work harder to catch up to the first-draft writing stage. In the process, even the most reluctant writers surprise themselves by being able to write a strong poem!

All writers need to do many rewrites. Published authors have often had to make changes fifty to sixty times before their text is printed. Publishers may make many suggestions for improvement, but the decision to change the text lies with the author. It may be tedious, but it does improve the final product! If you have an author visit coming up, or if you know an author who lives close by, ask the author to bring samples of his or her rewrites. It will show students that we all have to go through this stage.

The editing process should be firmly in the child's hands. This can be difficult sometimes because you may not always agree with the choices your students make. However, I do feel that this is one area in which the students can make their own decisions. Even if we don't like it, it doesn't mean that it's wrong! But making their own decisions during the writing process leads to a strong feeling of ownership, commitment, and pride in their work. Referring to children's ownership of a piece of writing, Dr. Donald Graves, says in Lucy McCormick Calkins' case study *Lessons from a Child*, "When people own a place, they look after it. When it belongs to someone else, they couldn't care less." Having the freedom to make their own decisions versus completing assigned topics with little or no choice gives the young author ownership in his or her writing.

Here is an example of how drastically a piece of writing can change, and improve, with some guidance. Angela, in grade 9, was writing prose. She told me that she didn't really like writing poetry. When I critiqued her story, I told her that her writing was very poetic and suggested she put the sentences in a little bit of different format. I showed her, on a sheet of paper, how her story changed when it took the shape of poetry.

This was the prose she had written:

> I remember that night I walked through the door to an
> empty house. I thought I was dreaming but I wasn't. I sat
> there for hours thinking of you, the hours we had, the days
> we spent running. Now you are gone, gone like the wind.
> I went to the door thinking it was you. I remember that
> night, that night without you.

I broke up her sentences and, after editing, this is the poem that Angela ended up with:

## That Night

*I remember that night*
*I walked through the door*
*to an empty house.*

*I thought I was dreaming,*
*a nightmare, but it wasn't . . .*

*I sat there for hours thinking of you*
*and the hours we had, the*
*days we spent running.*

*Now you are gone,*
*gone like the wind.*

*I went to the door*
*thinking it was you.*
*I remember that night*
*that first night without you.*

Incidentally, Angela told me the piece of writing was about the day her dog died. She loved, and was very proud of, the poem she realized she had written!

Another fun way to use peer editing is by explaining to your students the process in which published authors have their writing edited. The "author" can send a poem to the "publisher" (you), who then passes it on to an "editor" (another student). Once the editor is done, you can pass the poem back to the author who can use the editorial feedback during the rewriting process.

You can eventually take this a step further and assign the finished poem to an illustrator.

# Publishing and Sharing

## The Need for an Audience

Writers write so that readers can read. Audience is an essential element of writing. After all, the main purpose of writing is to have someone read your writing. The class is fine as audience for a while, but writers get excited about the prospect of new audiences. "Teachers need to struggle to find new audiences for their classes" (Mem Fox, *Radical Reflections*). So, when you have been writing poems with your students, you will want to share their accomplishments with others.

After a child goes through all the hard work of producing a good piece of writing, you can prevent them from saying, "Now what?" by offering opportunities to show their writing to the rest of the world. Whether it is publishing in the classroom or publishing online, by reading at an assembly or by sharing with parents, be sure to celebrate the accomplishment. Offer them a real audience!

## The Publishing Process

Once you start discussing various ways in which you can publish classroom books, it's a good idea to use this exercise to teach your students how books are published. Use and display the following books in your classroom to explain the process, from writing through editing and illustrating, to the final printed and bound product.

- *From Pictures to Words: A Book about Making a Book* by Janet Stevens
- *How a Book Is Made* by Aliki
- *Just Write!* by Sylvia Gunnery
- *Making a Picture Book* by Anne Bower Ingram
- *What Do Authors Do?* by Eileen Christelow
- *Write Now!* by Karleen Bradford
- *Writing Picture Books* by Kathy Stinson
- *Writing Your Best Picture Book Ever* by Kathy Stinson

## Designing and Illustrating Books

Once the editing process has been completed, help students produce a book of poems. A book not only showcases the poems, but also teaches students about the publishing process. When I do school visits, students are usually intrigued to learn how books are actually made. Most kids have no idea how books get printed or how they get illustrated. Creating awareness increases their interest. Besides, publishing your own book of poetry is fun! We'll talk here about producing a book on plain white paper that has a laminated cover, a spiral-coil binding, and illustrations.

You might want to state some criteria for selecting the poems and deciding on the number of poems to be included in the book. First, you'll need to decide if you will publish one book for each individual student-poet, or a classroom anthology (Of course, each student gets a copy).

When I complete a poetry workshop with students, I generally make one book for each individual student that includes their own poems that have made it through the critiquing and editing process. Each student's book will then include the whole spectrum of poems we have been writing: rhyming, non-rhyming, tongue twisters, poetry written to music, metaphors, and more.

But you might also decide to publish an anthology of selected work from the entire classroom. Your selection criterion might be to include samples of all formats of writing. Ask each student to submit two favorite poems. Be sure to give all students equal exposure.

## TYPEFACES

Your students first need to decide whether they want to produce a vertically oriented book (see Figure A), or one oriented horizontally (see Figure B). If the latter, remember to adjust the printer to print in the landscape mode. Also, make any illustrations run this way.

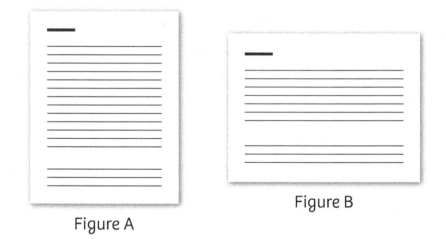

Figure B

Figure A

So, let's make books of poetry in the classroom. First, tell your students to type each poem on the computer and print one poem per sheet of paper. Show them their options: typefaces, sizes, spacing, etc., by printing one sample poem on a sheet of paper. The typeface in which it is printed has an effect on the visual impact of the poem. Let them experiment with different typefaces that enhance the contents of the poem, for example, bold, italic, ornate, small, and so on.

## ILLUSTRATIONS

Next, you can ask your students to decide what kind of illustrations to make with each poem. Illustrations can be made in color or black and white. Offer an assortment of markers, crayons, coloring pencils, and even paint. Computer graphics might be used, or you can use different forms of artwork, such as collage, Plasticine, or block printing. Combine this activity with any art form that suits your art curriculum. As in the writing process, allow students to plan, draft, and work on their illustrations on separate pieces of paper first.

Because a few children just "hate" doing their own pictures, I like to offer an option to draw their own illustrations by supplying them with a huge pile of book publishers' catalogues from which they can cut and paste illustrations and decorations. These catalogues have wonderful artwork. Book catalogues usually come out twice a year, in the spring and fall. Ask for them at any bookstore; they will gladly supply you with last season's catalogues.

You can give students the freedom to choose not to illustrate their books. Most professional authors do not illustrate their own work. "Real writers who can't paint don't illustrate their own stories. Kids who don't like drawing should not be made to illustrate their own writing" (Mem Fox, *Radical Reflections*). Many children—and adults—too, are surprised to learn that authors and illustrators do not necessarily work together at all. When a text is accepted for publication by a publisher, it becomes the publisher's responsibility to assign it to an illustrator. Two of my picture books have been illustrated by a wonderful illustrator whom I had never met. I never even talked to her on the phone. We finally met three years after the first book came out. In fact, while she was working on the illustrations, our publisher did not want us talking to each other!

You also may want to offer your students the option of having their writing illustrated by someone else. Why not let the kids ask someone in their class or in the school to illustrate their books? Students may have a brother who's very good at drawing or a friend who'd love to help out. Be sure to include the illustrator's name on the cover.

## COVERS

Students are now busy creating their illustrations, finishing the final drafts, or typing their stories on the computer. It's not a bad idea, at this time, to discuss covers for their books. Have a collection of books from the library on hand to show different covers. Choose some with attractive covers and some with what you consider to be boring covers. Try to find a variety of typefaces and colors.

Discuss with your students:

- What makes a cover attractive?
- What kind of illustration is on the cover?
- What does it tell you about the contents of the book?
- How big are the letters for title and author/illustrator names?

Ask your students to think about an attractive cover design. Do they have a catchy, attractive title for their poetry collection? It could be the name of one of the poems or any fun title. Alliterations sometimes work well for a book title.

Ask students to design a cover for their own books, complete with an illustration, a title, and the author's name. If you decide on an anthology, several students can work together to create the cover. Covers can be mounted on colored construction paper and then laminated.

To learn more about the publishing process, stop by your local newspaper or large printing business and ask for:

- samples of pages before they get cut. (Books and newspapers are not printed page by page but on huge sheets of paper.)

- color separations, to show students how books are printed in only four colors: cyan, magenta, yellow, and black. Look at any picture book or magazine with a magnifying glass to discover that all pictures are made up of dots of these four colors!

Most newspaper publishers use these items and throw them out after use. They make great classroom props. Even more fun: arrange for a field trip with your class to a local newspaper or book printer so your students can see the entire printing process.

## ABOUT THE AUTHOR

When producing books in the classroom, encourage your authors to write a page called "About the Author." This can include a short biographical write-up, as well as a photo. For examples, refer to bios on book jackets in the library. A photo can be pasted on a sheet of paper or you can use a digital camera to print it. Students may also choose to do a self-portrait. The students should decide whether they want this page, "About the Author," to be put on the outside of the back cover or inside the book. A class photograph works well for the anthology, and students can have fun writing a biography of their class. Again, giving them that choice makes the process much more exciting than compelling students to conform to one standard way of doing the books.

To complete designing the books, students can produce:

- a **title page**, showing just the title and the author's name in a typeface of their choice
- a **dedication page**, which can be to their best friend, their parents, or even their dog!
- an **index**, if applicable
- **book copy** (a summary of the book's contents) to paste on the back cover of their book, complete with an excerpt from one poem.
- a fictional **review**! "Ten weeks on the *New York Times* 'Best Sellers' list!"
- an **ISBN:** Every book in the world has its own ten- or thirteen-digit ISBN

(International Standard Book Number). ISBNs for the students' poetry books may be composed of birth dates, phone numbers, or secret codes.

- a **copyright** page, complete with the standard copyright warning and symbol. Refer inside any book for an example of the text, author name, dates, and copyright symbol. Look under "symbols" in your word processing program to find the icon. Use this activity to discuss how copyright protects an author's work.

## ASSEMBLING THE BOOKS

Give your students a file folder or large envelope to store their finished work. Make a checklist like this one for your students to help them complete the publishing process:

Name: _____

Check each item as you complete it. Keep your finished pages clean and flat.

- ☐ Make a cover, with title and author's name
- ☐ Print a dedication page
- ☐ Make several large illustrations for inside your book
- ☐ Print title page (just the title and your name)
- ☐ Print © page
- ☐ Print your poems, double-spaced, on numbered pages
- ☐ Print Table of Contents (optional)
- ☐ Print "About the Author" page with a photo

When everything is finished, pages should be carefully assembled. Ask each student to make sure pages are in the right order and right side up! Now the book is ready to be bound! To bind the books, I like using a plastic-coil binding. Most schools have a binding machine tucked away somewhere, but chances are that the students have never been allowed to use one. They'll find it fascinating to see how it works. If your school does not have one of these machines, an office-supply store can attach coil bindings for you for a small fee.

Other options to bind the books include using yarn, large staples, or a binder. You can also use a clear plastic cover with a spine that slides over the pages. Even a new cardstock folder can give a polished look to students' writing. You can also purchase ready-made blank books in which your students can write or paste poems and illustrations. The cover of a blank book can be colored and personalized.

> Make use of volunteer parents when you are ready to assemble and bind books.

# Book Launch

### PARENTS

Try to involve the parents with the writing activities as much as possible. This will also help to ensure their support of the child at home in reading and writing activities.

The crucial role of parents is confirmed by John Spink in his book, *Children as Readers*:

> "Parents have a central role to play in helping children to become competent readers. The partnership between teachers, parents, and children in reading programs has proved to be very successful—a mutually rewarding process involving encouragement of private reading, as well as public reading, book sharing, and book ownership."

When parents participate, the children will write in an atmosphere of greater support. When parents are part of the child's writing process, they become more aware of the different skills learned by the child while he or she is writing and rewriting and, usually, are more supportive of you because they have an understanding of what goes on in the classroom.

Because many parents work during the day and are unable to come to school, consider having the book launch during the lunch hour or in the evening. A special event often makes the students feel that their work is even more important and appreciated.

## PLANNING THE BOOK LAUNCH

Celebrate your students' achievements by throwing a party! All the writing, rewriting, word processing, illustrating, and binding have culminated into one big event: a book launch! Invite parents, grandparents, and siblings. Why not include your principal, district superintendent, school board members, or other special people who'd enjoy hearing your students' accomplishments? Another classroom could also be invited. You and your students should be proud of your accomplishments and might as well show off!

## INVITATIONS

Carefully consider the best time for the party and discuss it with your students. Ask some students to design an invitation on the computer. Someone else might contribute an illustration while yet two other students decide on the text. Be sure to include time, date, and place. You might want to ask parents to contribute to the fun by bringing cookies or juice. You may even want to design a rhyming invitation!

## PREP TIME

Before the event, explain that a book launch introduces a new book to readers. Encourage them to think about what they want to share about their own book of poetry. Tell your students you'd like them to talk to the audience about what gave them the idea to write these poems and to choose one or two of their favorite poems to read aloud.

If you have students who absolutely dread the idea of standing up in front of others to share, please don't force them. If anyone is truly uncomfortable, assure him or her that you won't call on that student but that, during the party, you can hold up that author's book and briefly mention some of its highlights. Once they see how well the others are received, they may lose their anxiety and decide to present their own writing!

During the book launch, the authors take turns speaking about their books and giving sample readings for the visitors. Many parents will have observed their child at home working on the book as he or she was engaged in the writing, but for others this will be the first time they hear some of the writing. In almost all instances, parents will be amazed at their child's ability to write and the wide variety of books produced.

When preparing to share poems out loud with an audience, help students to put expression and joy into their performance. A good resource to reference is poet Sara Holbrook's book:

- Sara Holbrook and Michael Salinger. *Outspoken! How to Improve Writing and Speaking Skills Through Poetry Performance*. Heinemann, 2006.

Sara says: "Call it poetic justice, but not only is performance poetry the hottest, hippest way for students to engage in literate behaviors, it's also an effective vehicle for helping students meet language arts standards. In fact, poetry performance meets eight of NCTE and IRA's twelve national standards for English instruction and contributes to the mastery of the other four."

In *Outspoken!* , The authors take students through the process of developing, implementing, and assessing poetry performance. Beginning with ideas for encouraging even the most reluctant students to speak clearly and write from the heart, they use workshop structures to guide young poets toward vibrant completed pieces and an exciting, dynamic delivery.

During a poetry performance or book launch, I have invited a local news reporter to take photos of the students and to interview the young authors. Having students' pictures in the paper because they wrote poems helps to generate excitement for writing. The entire writing process goes hand in hand with increased confidence and self-esteem.

> "Producing a finished product gives us not only the satisfaction of making something others can enjoy, but also, knowledge of the process. Children can learn a tremendous amount about how literature works by producing some."
>
> (Perry Nodelman, *The Pleasures of Children's Literature*)

At the conclusion of the readings, invite the audience to leaf through the displayed books and to visit with the authors. As a follow up, you may also consider asking the students to read from their books during a school assembly.

## More Ideas on Publishing in the Classroom:

- Produce books of poetry as a joint project with primary buddies.
- Your students can write for a younger audience. The younger children can add the illustrations.
- Poems and illustrations can also be designed with presentation software (like PowerPoint or Keynote) and published on the Internet with Google Docs. For an overview of this free and easy-to-manage resource, visit **www.google.com/google-d-s/tour1.html**.
- If poems are written by one person and illustrated by someone else, produce two copies. Show the name of the author and illustrator on the cover.
- A second copy of the book can be made for the school library, complete with barcode.

## Other Ways to Share and Celebrate

- To display poetry written by students, try a Poet Tree. Draw a huge tree with branches on a large sheet of brown or green paper. Cut out and tape to a wall in the school hallway or classroom.

- The students can write poems on leaf-shaped paper. (I use maple leaf-shaped notepads from educational supply stores.) Children can also spread one hand on a sheet of colored paper, trace it, and cut it out. Tape leaves with poems all over the tree. Poets sign the branches of their Poet Tree.
- Cut strips from colored construction paper. Ask students to write the title and author of each book or poem that they read on a strip of paper. Link pieces of paper together until you have a garland decoration for the classroom.
- Publish some of the poems in a school newsletter or submit them to your local community newspaper. Find out about Newspapers in Education and how you can make use of this national program (**www. naafoundation.org/Curriculum/NIE.aspx**).
- Invite each student to submit his or her best poem to you as the "publisher," and bind the collection into an anthology for classroom or school use. Knowing that you will keep and treasure their writing will make them feel honored.
- Use special occasions such as Children's Book Week or April 2nd (International Children's Book Day), to celebrate children's writing.
- Have students share their poetry by reciting it at a local seniors' home. Or contact your local radio station and discuss ways to have students read their writing on the air.
- Share outstanding poems by publishing them on your school's website, on a page of "Students' Writing." Illustrations can be scanned and posted as well.

## Submitting Poetry to Magazines

When you do have some outstanding poems, you can encourage your students to try to publish them in a magazine. Submitting writing to a magazine can be a time-consuming process and frustrating. But it is also enormously rewarding to see the poem in print!

This is how students should prepare:

- Decide which magazine is most suited for your poem. The editorial address will be inside.
- Send edited writing on clean, white paper and double-space it.
- Always include an S.A.S.E.—a self-addressed stamped envelope—with any writing you send to a publisher. Use an envelope your writing will fit in, buy an extra stamp that covers the cost to return it, and put it in with your story. If you live in the United States and you want to send your writing to Canada, you will need to have some Canadian stamps (and vice versa). Ask a relative or friend who is visiting or who lives in the country to bring some back for you.
- Write a cover letter to explain who you are and why you hope they will publish your poem.

Nowadays, many magazines have an online presence and accept submissions via e-mail. Some even prefer to work paperlessly, so check the guidelines on your favorite publications' websites before sending in any poems.

Magazines sometimes don't pay anything and sometimes they pay quite well ($75 for a short poem). If magazines want your story or poem, they will usually write you a letter and include a contract. They will send you a check and a copy of the magazine once they publish your work. Once you start submitting your writing to book publishers or to magazines, prepare yourself for rejections. Every writer gets them! Dr. Seuss had his first book rejected twenty-seven times! However, Gordon Korman had his first book accepted for publication when he was in seventh grade.

## MAGAZINES THAT PUBLISH WRITING BY CHILDREN

Please note that this is not an all-inclusive list.

*OWL* and *Chickadee*
56 The Esplanade, Suite 304
Toronto, Ontario M5E 1A7, Canada

*Highlights For Children* ("Our Own Pages")
803 Church Street
Honesdale, PA 18431

*Stone Soup* (a magazine by and for children under thirteen)
Editor
P.O. Box 83
Santa Cruz, CA 95063
or **http://www.stonesoup.com**.

See also the list of online writing sites at the end of this chapter.

## Publishing on the Internet

Another way to give your students an audience is by making use of the World Wide Web! It is already there, waiting for you to share. In most cases, it's free—and it's a lot faster and easier than publishing in print. School websites can be used to post students' poetry.

Sometimes, parents and teachers are hesitant to use the Internet, fearing that children won't read books when they use technology. But when children spend time online, they are often reading and writing. When children communicate with others around the world via e-mail, instant messaging, or through social networking sites, they are reading and writing for a real purpose. When children find information on the Web, they read. When a student posts a message that can be read by thousands, he or she is conscious of spelling and makes sure that it is done correctly.

In fact, it has been said that the art of letter writing, as well as the ancient tradition of storytelling, is making a comeback through technology. Computers offer these opportunities.

However, computers never could, or should replace a teacher as mentor or act as a substitute for human dialogue in guiding students. Test results,

Reluctant to try computer technology? Read *The Connected Family: Bridging the Digital Generation Gap* by Seymour Papert.

however, show that a hands-on approach with computers is an extraordinarily rich means of learning, across a wide range of cognitive and behavioral styles. In fact, many children said to have been disabled flourish in a hands-on environment.

Integrating technology into classroom practices uses these valuable resources in a more effective manner and offers alternative learning styles to children. Find ways to make computer lab time relevant and authentic by giving students writing activities to follow up on from the classroom.

By using word processors and printers, students can make their books look good. They can print covers and title pages, scan a photo of the author, and put a real copyright symbol on their work.

Using e-mail to teach writing gives a student both practice using of the Internet and a professional with which to consult. Not only do students benefit from this form of communication, but e-mail allows me, as a mentor, to work and connect with children when it suits me—rather than having to be in a classroom at a set time. It also allows the child to write independently and in privacy, away from peers who might influence the child if writing was done as a shared classroom activity.

I created an e-mail writing program after I visited a seventh grade class in a school in a small community. After writing poetry all afternoon, a burly seventh grader in a leather jacket sauntered over to me, handed me a crumpled up piece of paper, and mumbled, "Don't look at it until you've left." Which I did. I found a beautiful, sensitive poem and realized this is the kind of writer I wanted to reach: a student who doesn't want his peers to know he really likes, and grows from, writing. E-mail allows me to reach these kids.

## CONNECTING WITH AN AUDIENCE

An online magazine, or e-zine, in which children can see their writing published allows for a faster turnover of contents and is much less costly to produce than a printed magazine. An e-zine allows students to share their writing easily with an audience around the world and offers an opportunity to read writing by peers. Other children can comment, give feedback, get ideas for their own writing, and generally help a young author grow as a writer and as a reader. Children anywhere can read each other's stories, generate ideas, use their imaginations, and improve their vocabulary and spelling while doing so. Reading and writing will be done with a real purpose.

## PUBLISHING AN E-ZINE

A simple computer with modem and space on a server are all that you need to create your own Web magazine. If your school already has its own website, you may choose to use this as the place to post your students' writing. Ask your school's technology coordinator for help.

If you are going to post your students' stories on the Internet, here are some recommendations:

- focus on writing
- make it a simple, easy-to-use website
- add links to related sites
- include stories, poems, and perhaps even illustrations
- publish only the student-poets' first names
- obtain parental consent if needed and make sure that the posted personal information complies with the rules in your school or district
- use a limited number of —or lower resolution—graphics so download time is fast

Most word processing programs allow you to post stories directly in HTML. The technology coordinator should also be able to assist you in creating the webpages if you need help. If no technology consultant is available, try a high school student! Sometimes they can help you with your problems and earn credit at the same time.

The first page on a website, the home page, is usually an introduction to the school with links to related pages of information. You can create a new link with a button that says something like "Students' Poems" or "Our Published Pages." When readers click on this button, it will take them to the pages of stories your students have created.

Type the children's writing on your computer, or simply transfer it onto your computer from their files, and then upload the files to the server. You can use any kind of webpage software for this purpose.

I have posted writing on the Internet by children who participated in writing workshops that I conducted in different schools. After their stories and poems were posted, students and teachers visited the website to critique its usability and contents. I discussed the online magazine's relevancy, practical use, contents, etc., with children because I wanted to find out how each student viewed the site in relation to his or her own writing.

Students participating in these discussions came from grades 4 through 8. Their feedback was interesting. When discussing how the use of this website would relate to their own writing, students' comments included the following:

- "I liked knowing that some of the poems were read by people locally and others were from far away."
- "It helped me to get ideas from reading other students' writing."
- "Reading other children's writing shows how different everyone writes. It's fun."
- "I liked to see what ideas other children had used."

Most students felt that reading the e-zine would be helpful to their own writing, both in reading other people's writing and in getting ideas. Most felt that knowing a website was available would encourage them to write more. Invariably, students commented that they enjoyed reading other students' writing. They commented on the value of seeing their writing published:

"Sometimes I read someone else's poem, and it inspires me to write my own. Reading [a site like this] encourages me to write."

- "If the poem I wrote was really good, I would want to submit it to be published on a website. Knowing that your story or poem was to be published would be exciting."
- "I would love to publish a poem to show other children that I can write, too."
- "It's much easier to read an online magazine than having to buy one."
- "It is too cumbersome to submit writing to a regular magazine."

All students felt that friends, parents, and relatives would want to read their writing once it was published online.

I was surprised that none of the children mentioned that being published online would somehow be less impressive than to have writing published in a printed magazine. When no one raised this issue, I eventually asked the children if they felt it to be less "real" to be published on the Internet as compared to being published in a printed magazine. The children strongly disagreed, saying that it would be much better to be published online "because then everyone can read it."

Using computers and connectivity allows students to develop skills necessary in other areas of their education, as well as in their future endeavors. Perhaps we can apply the enthusiasm children show for computer and video games and help them to direct it towards writing. By having a place to post and share their writing, children will write more, enjoy doing so, and be proud of their accomplishments.

# Chapter 5: Bibliography and Websites

## BIBLIOGRAPHY

Aliki. *How A Book Is Made.* New York: Harper Trophy, 1988.

Bradford, Karleen. *Write Now! How to Turn Your Ideas into Great Stories.* Markham, Ont.: Scholastic Canada, 1996.

Christelow, Eileen. *What Do Authors Do?* New York: Clarion Books, 1995.

Fox, Mem. *Radical Reflections: Passionate Opinions on Teaching, Learning, and Living.* New York: Mariner Books, 1993.

Gunnery, Sylvia. *Just Write! Ten Practical Workshops for Successful Student Writing.* Markham, Ont.: Pembroke Publishers, 1998.

Ingram, Anne Bower. *Making a Picture Book.* North Ryde, N.S.W.: Methuen Australia, 1987.

Nodelman, Perry. *The Pleasures of Children's Literature.* New York: Longman Publishing Group, 1992.

Papert, Seymour. *The Connected Family: Bridging the Digital Generation Gap.* Atlanta: Longstreet Press, 1996.

Spink, John. *Children as Readers: A Study.* London: Clive Bingley, 1989.

Stevens, Janet. *From Pictures to Words: A Book About Making a Book.* New York: Holiday House, 1995.

Stinson, Kathy. *Writing Picture Books: What Works and What Doesn't.* Markham, Ont.: Pembroke Publishers, 1991.

Stinson, Kathy. *Writing Your Best Picture Book Ever.* Markham, Ont.: Pembroke Publishers, 1994.

## WEBSITES

To view an extensive list of online publishing resources for students, visit the Children's Literature Web Guide: **http://www.acs.ucalgary.ca/~dkbrown/writings.html**.

The American Library Association maintains a website full of links to great children's sites. Many of these are book and poetry related. To view the list, go to: **http://www.ala.org/gwstemplate.cfm?section=greatwebsites&te**

mplate=/cfapps/gws/displaysection.cfm&sec=18.

For a reading motivation program for children in grades K-8 that lets children create their own reading lists, visit the Book Adventure by going to: **http://www.bookadventure.org**.

The Canadian Children's Book Centre (CCBC) is a national, not-for-profit organization dedicated to encouraging, promoting and supporting the reading, writing, illustrating and publishing of Canadian books for young readers. For resources for teachers from the CCBC, go to: **http://www.bookcentre.ca**.

Cyberkids is an online children's site which offers, among other things, a place to share stories and poetry. To view the poetry section, go to: **http://www.cyberkids.com/cw/poe**.

The Horn Book Magazine is a publication about children's and young adult literature. To learn more, go to: **http://www.hbook.com**.

For a podcast about children's books, complete with interviews by many authors, visit the Just One More Book website: **http://www.justonemorebook.com**.

Kidpub is a site of books and stories written by children. To read the stories or to post your own, go to: **http://www.kidpub.com**.

To give kids an opportunity to see their writing published on the Internet, visit the KidLit website by going to:  **http://mgfx.com/kidlit**.

*New Moon Girls* is an online community and magazine where girls create and share, among other things, poetry. To view the website, go to: **http://www.newmoon.org**.

For a useful site dedicated to poets and poetry, visit the Poetry Foundation website: **http://www.poetryfoundation.org**.

*Stone Soup* is a literary print magazine written and illustrated by young writers and artists. To subscribe, view samples, or learn more about the publication, go to: **http://www.stonesoup.com**.

To view lists of writing resources for students, visit the Wordwright's Writing Resources for Students webpage: **http://www3.sympatico.ca/susanio/WWCcomp.html#publish**.

Writing with Writers (Scholastic) allows students to listen to poets as well as create their own poems. To visit the site, go to: **http://teacher.scholastic.com/writewit/poetry**.

*The Claremont Review* is a magazine that showcases inspiring young adult writers. To view samples or to subscribe, go to: **www.theclaremontreview.ca**.

For unusual events that can spark stories or poems, go to *USA Today*'s Weird News section: **http://www.usatoday.com/news/offbeat/default.htm**.

The International Board on Books for Young People (IBBY) is a non-profit organization which represents an international network of people from all over the world who are committed to bringing books and children together. For more information, go to: **http://www.ibby.org**.

For the Canadian and US sections of this organization, go to: **http://www.ibby-canada.org** and **http://www.usbby.org**.

Wet Ink is an arts magazine for and by Canadian youth that is no longer in publication. The magazine is currently offering manuscript evaluation for a short time. To view the last issue or to submit work, go to: **http://www.wetinkmagazine.com**.

## Treasure Chest

*Open the cover of the book in your hands,*
*bridge to unknown and wonderful lands.*
*Travel through countries of wisdom and fun,*
*nights full of darkness, days full of sun.*

*Turn each page full of wonder,*
*follow its road to up yonder*
*where mountain tops talk to the sky*
*whispering a wondering "why"?*

*Treasure chest of make-believe places,*
*meeting new and familiar faces. Reach*
*for a book on the shelf—*
*Discover the world, discover yourself.*

(Margriet Ruurs)

It's my hope that this book has helped you find some new activities and some new ways in which to help your students discover—first and foremost—the joy of writing poetry. I hope it wasn't a one-time experience and that you will keep writing and using poetry throughout your day, every day of your teaching.

Whether you publish the poems or post them on the Internet, share them with other students or parents, I hope you will instill a lifelong love of poetry in your students.

I suggest that you join your state or provincial IRA (the International Reading Association) to discover more great literature and to meet writers at annual conferences. But most of all, savor poetry each and every day!

# Classroom Poems

*I live in fear*
*that I*
*will teach the poem*
*and they*
*will lose the poet*
*and the song and*
*the self*
*within the poem.*

*I live in fear*
*that I*
*who love the poem*
*and the children*
*will lose the poem*
*and the children*
*when I teach the poem.*

*But I will teach the poem*
*Live with the fear*
*Love the children*
*Sing the song*
*Find the self*
*And know the poet is*
*beside me*
*Just as afraid*
*But full of hope.*

(David Booth, *Poems Please*)

# Bibliography

Adoff, Arnold. *Black Is Brown Is Tan.* New York: HarperCollins, 1987.

Adoff, Arnold, and Jerry Pinkney. *In for Winter, Out for Spring.* New York: Harcourt, 1997.

Adoff, Arnold, and John Steptoe. *Outside Inside Poems.* New York: Voyager Picture Books, 1995.

Ahlberg, Janet and Allan Ahlberg. *The Jolly Postman: Or Other People's Letters.* London: Heinemann, 1986.

Allinson, Beverley. *Effie.* New York: Scholastic, 1997.

Bagert, Brod. *Chicken Socks: And Other Contagious Poems.* Honesdale, Penn.: Boyds Mills Press, 2000.

Bagert, Brod. *Let Me Be the Boss: Poems for Kids to Perform.* Honesdale, Penn.: Boyds Mills Press, 1992.

Bagert, Brod. *Rainbows, Head Lice, and Pea-Green Tile: Poems in the Voice of the Classroom Teacher.* Gainesville, Fla.: Maupin House Publishing, 1999.

Baker, Jeannie. *The Window*. Walker Books, 2002.

Bannatyne-Cugnet, *Jo. A Prairie Alphabet*. Tundra, 2009.

Banyai, Istvan. *Zoom.* Puffin, 1998.

Base, Graeme. *Animalia*, New York: Harry N. Abrams, 1986.

Base, Graeme. *The Eleventh Hour.* Don Mills, Ont.: Stoddart Publishing, 1988.

Base, Graeme. *The Sign of the Seahorse: A Tale of Greed and High Adventure in Two Acts.* New York: Harry N. Abrams, 1992.

Base, Graeme. *The Water Hole.* New York: Harry N. Abrams, 2001.

Base, Graeme. *The Worst Band in the Universe.* Toronto: Doubleday Canada, 1999.

Bauer, Carolyn Feller. *Halloween: Stories & Poems.* New York: HarperCollins, 1992.

Bauer, Carolyn Feller. *Valentine's Day: Stories and Poems.* New York: HarperCollins, 1993.

Bogart, Jo Ellen. *Gifts.* Markham, Ont.: Scholastic Canada, 1996.

Booth, David. *Voices on the Wind: Poems for all Seasons.* Toronto: Kids Can Press, 1990.

Booth, David. *Images of Nature: Canadian Poets and the Group of Seven.* Kids Can Press, 1995.

Brett, Jan. *The Mitten.* Putnam, 2009.

Brown, Marc. *Scared Silly! A Book for the Brave.* Boston: Little Brown and Co., 1994.

Bryant, Ashley. *Ashley Bryan's ABC of African American Poetry.* New York: Atheneum, 1997.

Burleigh, Robert. *Hoops.* San Diego: Harcourt Brace, 1997.

Carroll, Lewis. *Jabberwocky.* New York: Harry N. Abrams. 1989

Cole, Joanna and Stephanie Calmensen. *Six Sick Sheep:101 Tongue Twisters.* William Morrow & Co, 1993

Conford, Ellen. *A Royal Pain.* Point, 1990.

Crossley-Holland, Kevin. *Once Upon a Poem.* Chicken House Ltd, 2005.

Dahl, Roald. *Ronald Dahl's Revolting Rhymes.* London: Puffin Books, 1982.

Day, David, and Aska Warabé. *Aska's Animals.* Toronto: Doubleday Canada, 1991.

Feelings, Tom, and Eloise Greenfield. *Daydreamers.* New York: E. P. Dutton, 1993.

Feelings, Tom. *Soul Looks Back in Wonder.* New York: Dial Books, 1993.

Fitch, Sheree. *If You Could Wear My Sneakers! A Book About Children's Rights.* Toronto: Doubleday Canada, 1997.

Fitch, Sheree. *Sleeping Dragons All Around.* Toronto: Doubleday Canada, 1989.

Fitch, Sheree. *There Were Monkeys in My Kitchen.* Toronto: Doubleday Canada, 1992.

Fitch, Sheree. *There's a Mouse in My House.* Toronto: Doubleday Canada, 1997.

Fitch, Sheree. *Toes in My Nose: And Other Poems.* Toronto: Doubleday Canada, 1987.

Franco, Betsy. *Math Poetry, Linking Language & Math in a Fresh Way*. Good Year Books, 2006).

Franco, Betsy. *Mathematickles*. McElderry, 2006.

Granfield, Linda. *High Flight: A Story of World War II.* Tundra, 1999.

Granfield, Linda. *In Flanders Fields: The Story of the Poem by John McCrae.* Tundra, 2005.

Granfield, Linda. *Amazing Grace: The Story of the Hymn. Tundra,* 2001.

Granfield, Linda. *Silent Night, The Song from Heaven*. Tundra, 2000.

Goldstein, Bobbye S. *Bear in Mind: A book of Bear Poems.* New York: Viking Kestrel, 1989.

Goldstein, Bobbye S. *What's on the Menu?* New York: Viking Juvenile, 1992.

Harley, Avis. *Fly with Poetry: An ABC of Poetry.* Honesdale, Penn.: Boyds Mill Press, 2000.

Holbrook, Sara. *By Definition*, Boyd's Mills Press.

Holbrook, Sara and Michael Salinger. *High Definition*. Heinemann, 2010.

Holbrook, Sara and Michael Salinger. *Outspoken! How to Improve Writing and Speaking Skills Through Poetry Performance*. Heinemann, 2006.

Hopkins, Lee Bennett. *Dinosaurs.* Orlando: Harcourt Brace, 1987.

Hopkins, Lee Bennett. *More Surprises* (an "I Can Read Book"). New York: Harper & Row, 1987.

Hopkins, Lee Bennett. *Extra Innings: Baseball Poems.* Orlando: Harcourt Brace, 1993.

Hopkins, Lee Bennett. *Good Morning to You, Valentine: Poems for Valentine's Day*. HBJ, 1976

Hopkins, Lee Bennett. *Marvelous Math: A Book of Poems*. Simon & Schuster, 2001.

Hopkins, Lee Bennett. *Spectacular Science: A Book of Poems*. Simon & Schuster, 2002.

Hopkins, Lee Bennett. *Got Geography*. Greenwillow Books, 2006.

Ichikawa, Satomi, and Cynthia Mitchell. *Under the Cherry Tree.* New York: William Collins, 1979.

Katz, Bobbi. *Truck Talk: Rhymes on Wheels.* New York: Scholastic, 1997.

Kellogg, Steven. *Aster Aardvark's Alphabet Adventures.* New York: Morrow Junior Books, 1987.

Kellogg, Steven. *There Was an Old Woman.* New York: Four Winds Press, 1987.

Kennedy, Dorothy M. *Make Things Fly: Poems about the Wind.* New York: Margaret K. McElderry Books, 1998.

Knowles, Sheena. *Edward the Emu.* HarperCollins, 1998.

Korman, Gordon, and Bernice Korman. *The D- Poems of Jeremy Bloom: A Collection of Poems About School, Homework, and Life.* New York: Scholastic, 1992.

Korman, Gordon, and Bernice Korman. *The Last Place Sports Poems of Jeremy Bloom: A Collection of About Winning, Losing, and Being a Good Sport (Sometimes).* New York: Scholastic, 1996.

Lansky, Bruce. *A Bad Case of the Giggles: Kid's Favorite Funny Poems.* New York: Meadowbrook Press, 1994.

Lansky, Bruce. *Poetry Party.* New York: Meadowbrook Press, 1996.

Layne, Steven. *The Principal's Night Before Christmas.* Pelican Publishing, 2004.

Layne, Steven. *Teacher's Night Before Christmas.* Pelican Publising, 2001.

Lear, Edward. *The Complete Nonsense of Edward Lear.* New York: Dover Publications, 1951.

Lee, Dennis. *Alligator Pie.* Toronto: Macmillan of Canada, 1974.

Lee, Dennis. *Garbage Delight.* Toronto: Macmillan of Canada, 1979.

Lee, Dennis. *The Ice Cream Store.* New York: HarperCollins, 1991.

Lee, Dennis. *Jelly Belly.* Toronto: Macmillan of Canada, 1983.

Lesynski, Loris. *Catmagic.* Toronto: Annick Press, 1998.

Lesynski, Loris. *Nothing Beats a Pizza.* Annick, 2001.

Lesynski, Loris and Michael Martchenko. *I Did It Because, How A Poem Happens.* Annick, 2006.

Lewis, J. Patrick. *The Bookworm's Feast: A Potluck of Poems.* New York: Dial Books, 1999.

Lewis, J. Patrick. *July is a Mad Mosquito.* New York: Atheneum, 1994.

Little, Jean. *I Know an Old Laddie.* New York: Viking Children's Books, 1999.

Little, Jean. *I Gave My Mom a Castle.* Orca Book Publishers, 2003.

Livingston, Myra Cohn. *Celebrations.* New York: Holiday House, 1985.

Livingston, Myra Cohn. *Christmas Poems.* New York: Holiday House, 1988.

Livingston, Myra Cohn. *A Circle of Seasons.* New York: Holiday House, 1982.

Livingston, Myra Cohn. *Easter Poems.* New York: Holiday House, 1989.

Livingston, Myra Cohn. *Halloween Poems.* New York: Holiday House, 1989.

Livingston, Myra Cohn. *Festivals*. Holiday House, 1996.

Manning, Linda. *Animal Hours*. Fitzhenry & Whiteside, 2002.

Martin Jr., Bill, and John Archambault. *Barn Dance!* New York: Henry Holt, 1986.

Mathis, Sharon Bell. *Red Dog, Blue Fly: Football Poems*. New York: Viking, 1991.

McFarlane, Sheryl. *Jessie's Island*. Orca, 2002.

Mortenson, Greg. *Listen to the Wind*. Dial, 2009.

Moore, Clement Clarke. *The Night Before Christmas.* Buffalo: Firefly Books, 1999.

Murphy, Sally. *Pearl Verses The World.* Sydney: Walker Books Australia, 2009.

O'Huigin, Sean. *The Ghost Horse of the Mounties.* Windsor, Ont.: Black Moss Press, 1983.

O'Huigin, Sean. *I'll Belly Your Button in a Minute!* Windsor, Ont.: Black Moss Press, 1985.

O'Huigin, Sean. *Pickles and the Dog Nappers*. Windsor, Ont.: Black Moss Press, 1986.

Okutoro, Lydia. *Quiet Storm, Voices of Young Black Poets.* New York: Hyperion Books, 1999.

Ormerod, Jan. *Sunshine*. Frances Lincoln Children's Books, 2009.

Pappas, Theoni. *Adventures of Penrose the Mathematical Cat*. Wide World Publishing, 1997

Pappas, Theoni. *Fractals, Googols, and Other Mathematical Tales.* Wide World Publishing, 1993.

Paulsen, Gary. *Hatchet*. Simon & Schuster, 2007

Pearson, *Kit. Awake and Dreaming*. Penguin, 2008.

Peet, Bill. *Huge Harold.* Boston: Houghton Mifflin, 1961.

Peet, Bill. *The Whingdingdilly.* Boston: Houghton Mifflin, 1970.

Pinczes, Elinor J. *A Remainder of One*. Sandpiper, 2002.

Pomerantz, Charlotte. *If I Had a Paka.* New York: Greenwillow Books, 1993.

Prelutsky, Jack. *For Laughing Out Loud: Poems to Tickle Your Funnybone.* New York: Alfred A. Knopf, 1991.

Prelutsky, Jack. *A Pizza the Size of the Sun.* New York: Greenwillow Books, 1996.

Prelutsky, Jack. *Ride A Purple Pelican.* New York: Greenwillow Books, 1986.

Prelutsky, Jack. *Ride a Purple Pelican*, taped edition. Music by Michael Isaacson, Listening Library, 1988.

Prelutsky, Jack. *The Sheriff of Rottenshot.* New York: Greenwillow Books, 1982.

Prelutsky, Jack. *Something Big Has Been Here.* New York: Scholastic, 1992.

Prelutsky, Jack. *Tyrannosaurus Was a Beast.* New York: Greenwillow Books, 1988.

Seuss, Dr. and Jack Prelutsky. *Hooray for Diffendoofer Day!* New York: Knopf Books for Young Readers, 1998.

Reid, Barbara. *Two by Two.* Toronto: North Winds Press, 1992.

Reid, Barbara. *The Party.* Markham, Ont.: Scholastic Canada, 1997.

Remkiewicz, Frank and Patrick J. Lewis. *Scien-Trickery: Riddles in Science.* Sandpiper, 2007

Ruurs, Margriet. *Animal Alphabed.* Boyds Mills Press, 2005

Ruurs, Margriet. *A Pacific Alphabet*, Whitecap, 2001

Ruurs, Margriet. *A Mountain Alphabet.* Toronto: Tundra Books, 1996.

Ruurs, Margriet. *Virtual Maniac: Silly and Serious Poems for Kids.* Gainesville, Fla.: Maupin House Publishing, 2000.

Ruurs, Margriet. *In My Backyard.* Tundra, 2007.

Schertle, Alice. *A Lucky Thing.* Scholastic, 2001.

Schmidt, Gary D. *Poetry for Young People: Robert Frost.* Sterling, 2008.

Schwartz, David M. *If You Made a Million*. HarperCollins,1994.

Service, Robert. *The Best of Robert Service.* Toronto: McGraw Hill, 1971.

Service, Robert. *The Cremation of Sam McGee.* Toronto: Kids Can Press, 2006.

Service, Robert. *The Shooting of Dan McGrew.* Toronto: Kids Can Press, 1988.

Seuss, Dr. and Jack Prelutsky. *Hooray for Diffendoofer Day!* New York: Knopf Books for Young Readers, 1998.

Seuss, Dr. *I Can Read with My Eyes Shut.* New York: Random House, 1978.

Seuss, Dr. *Oh, the Places You'll Go.* New York: Random House, 1990.

Seuss, Dr. *Yertle the Turtle.* New York: Random House, 1950.

Scieszka , Jon. *Science Verse.* New York: Viking Juvenile, 2004.

Silverstein, Shel. *Falling Up.* New York: HarperCollins, 1996.

Singer, Marilyn. *Sky Words.* New York: Macmillan Publishing, 1994.

Schiltz, Laura Amy. *Good Masters! Sweet Ladies! Voices from a Medieval Village.* Somerville, Mass.: Candlewick, 2008.

Spinelli, Eileen. *Polar Bear, Arctic Hare: Poems of the Frozen North.* Wordsong, 2007.

Tang, Greg. *The Grapes of Math.* Scholastic, 2004.

Tang, Greg. *Math-terpieces.* Scholastic, 2003.

*The Candlewick Book of First Rhymes.* Cambridge, Mass.: Candlewick Press, 1996.

Vaccaro Seeger, Laura. *What If?* Roaring Brook Press, 2010

Viorst, Judith. *The Alphabet from Z to A (With Much Confusion on the Way).* New York, Atheneum, 1994.

Waldron, Kathleen Cook. *A Winter's Yarn.* Red Dear, Alta.: Red Deer College Press, 1986.

Woolger, David. *The Magic Tree.* Toronto: Oxford University Press, 1987.

Yolen, Jane. *Alphabestiary: Animal Poems from A to Z.* Honesdale, Penn.: Boyds Mills Press, 1995.

Yolen, Jane. *Best Witches, Poems for Halloween.* New York: G.P. Putnam's Sons, 1989.

Yolen, Jane. *Color Me a Rhyme: Nature Poems for Young People.* Honesdale, Penn.: Boyds Mills Press, 2000.

Yolen, Jane. *Mouse's Birthday.* New York: G. P. Putnam's Sons, 1993.

Yolen, Jane. *Owl Moon.* New York: Scholastic, 1987.

Yolen, Jane. *Sea Watch.* New York: Philomel Books, 1996.

Yolen, Jane. *Snow, Snow: Winter Poems for Children.* Honesdale, Penn.: Boyds Mills Press, 1998.

Yolen, Jane. *Street Rhymes Around the World.* Honesdale, Penn.: Boyds Mills Press, 1992.

Zolotow, Charlotte. *When the Wind Stops.* HarperCollins, 1997.

## OTHER RELEVANT BOOKS

Jarrell, Randall. *The Bat-Poet.* New York: HarperCollins, 1997.

Lear, Edward. *The Complete Nonsense of Edward Lear.* New York: Dover Publications, 1951.

Lewis, J. Patrick. *Spot the Plot: A Riddle Book of Book Riddles.* San Francisco: Chronicle Books, 2009.

Stevenson, Robert Louis. *A Child's Garden of Verses.* Don Mills, Ont.: Oxford University Press, 1966.

Vaughan, Marcia K. *Wombat Stew.* Englewood Cliffs, N.J.: Silver Burdett Press, 1986.

Weidt, Maryann N. *Oh, the Places He Went.* Minneapolis: Carolrhoda Books, 1994.

Young, Sue. *The Scholastic Rhyming Dictionary.* New York: Scholastic, 1997.

## BOOKS FOR TEACHERS

Booth, David. *Classroom Voices.* Toronto: Harcourt Brace, 1994.

Booth, David. *Literacy Techniques: For Building Successful Readers and Writers.* Markham, Ont.: Pembroke Publishers, 1996.

Booth, David, and Bill Moore. *Poems Please! Sharing Poetry with Children.* Markham, Ont. Pembroke Publishers, 1988.

Brownlie, Faye, Susan Close, and Linda Wingren. *Reaching for Higher Thought: Reading, Writing, Thinking Strategies.* Edmonton, Alberta: Arnold Publishing, 1988.

Brownlie, Faye, Susan Close, and Linda Wingren. *Tomorrow's Classroom Today: Strategies for Creating Active Readers, Writers, and Thinkers.* Portsmouth, N.H.: Heinemann, 1990.

Buzzeo, Toni, and Jane Kurtz. *Terrific Connections with Authors, Illustrators and Storytellers: Real Space and Virtual Links.* Westport, Conn.: Libraries Unlimited, 1999.

Calkins, Lucy McCormick. *Lessons from a Child: On the Teaching and Learning of Writing.* Portsmouth, N.H.: Heinemann, 1983.

Esbensen, Barbara Juster. *A Celebration of Bees: Helping Children Write Poetry.* New York: Henry Holt, 1995. (Can only be ordered from: tory@ttinet.com or 612-929-2065.)

Fox, Mem. *Radical Reflections: Passionate Opinions on Teaching, Learning, and Living.* New York: Mariner Books, 1993.

Freeman, Marcia S. *Building a Writing Community: A Practical Guide.* Gainesville, FL: Maupin House Publishing, 1997.

Goforth, Frances S. *Literature & the Learner.* New York: Wadsworth Publishing Company, 1998.

Heitman, Jane. *Teach Writing to Older Readers Using Picture Books: Every Picture Tells a Story.* Linworth, 2005.

Hodges, John C., Robert K. Miller, and Mary E. Whitten. *Harbrace College Handbook.* New York: HBJ, 1986.

Hopkins, Lee Bennett. *Pass the Poetry Please!* HarperCollins, 1998.

Jobe, Ron, and Mary Dayton-Sakari. *Reluctant Readers: Connecting Students and Books for Successful Reading Experiences.* Markham, Ont.: Pembroke Publishers, 1999.

Jobe, Ron, and Paula Hart. *Canadian Connections: Experiencing Literature with Children.* Markham, Ont.: Pembroke Publishers, 1991.

Moore, William H., *Words That Taste Good: More than 600 Short, Sharp, Sparkling Bits of Poetry.* Markham, Ont.: Pembroke Publishers, 1987.

Nodelman, Perry. *The Pleasures of Children's Literature.* New York: Longman Publishing Group, 1992.

Papert, Seymour. *The Connected Family: Bridging the Digital Generation Gap.* Atlanta: Longstreet Press, 1996.

Spink, John. *Children as Readers: A Study.* London: Clive Bingley, 1989.

## BOOKS FOR KIDS ABOUT WRITING

Aliki. *How A Book Is Made.* New York: Harper Trophy, 1988.

Bradford, Karleen. *Write Now! How to Turn Your Ideas into Great Stories.* Markham, Ont.: Scholastic Canada, 1996.

Christelow, Eileen. *What Do Authors Do?* New York: Clarion Books, 1995.

Ellis, Sarah. *The Young Writer's Companion.* Toronto: Groundwood Press, 1999.

Gunnery, Sylvia. *Just Write! Ten Practical Workshops for Successful Student Writing.* Markham, Ont.: Pembroke Publishers, 1998.

Ingram, Anne Bower. *Making a Picture Book.* North Ryde, N.S.W.: Methuen Australia, 1987.

Lesynski, Loris. *"I Did It Because …" How A Poem Happens* . Toronto: Annick Press, 2006.

Rubins, Diane Teitel. *Scholastic's A+ Guide to Good Writing.* New York: Scholastic, 1986.

Stevens, Janet. *From Pictures to Words: A Book About Making a Book.* New York: Holiday House, 1995.

Stinson, Kathy. *Writing Picture Books: What Works and What Doesn't.* Markham, Ont.: Pembroke Publishers, 1991.

Stinson, Kathy. *Writing Your Best Picture Book Ever.* Markham, Ont.: Pembroke Publishers, 1994.

# Index

**A**
Acrostic........................ 104, 108
About the author ...... 135-136
Alliteration........ 19, 46, 84, 91
Art......................................26, 133
Audience ....... 08, 17, 130, 145

**B**
Book launch................ 137-141

**C**
Choice........................14-15, 127
Covers .......................... 134-135
Critiquing................... 124-127

**D**
Diamante .................... 111-113

**E**
Editing...................53, 124-129
ESL...............................................06
E-zine ........................... 145-147

**F**
Found poems...................81-82

**I**
Illustration..26, 28, 72, 131, 133
International Reading
Association............................. 152

**L**
Language arts ...09-10, 25, 139
Loop poetry ................ 113-115

**M**
Magazines.......... 141-143, 145
Math...................... 24, 101-102
Memorizing .....................94-95
Metaphor .................. 20, 60-62
Music ................... 25-26, 55-58

**N**
Narrative poems............58-59
Nature poems .................54-55
Newspaper file ...............29-31
Newspapers...........................141
Non-rhyming poetry.....49-53

**P**
Peer conferencing .... 126-129
Personification... 20, 103-104
Personal favorites ................68
Physical education...............25
Picture file ................ 28-29, 72
Poet tree...................... 140-141
Poetic language.............. 02, 19
Poetry box ...............................27
Publishing online ....... 145-147
Puzzle ........................... 108-111

**R**
Reading aloud.................14-15
Reflective poetry ...... 105-107
Rhyme schemes ..........., 20-22
Rhyming dictionary ...42, 123
Rhythm ..............................48-49
Role of parents ..67, 95, 137-138

**S**
Science........................112, 116
Seasons.............................96-98
Senses ....................... 54, 76-80
Shapes...............................91-93
Simile......................... 20, 63-64
Special needs ..................06-07
Standards.........09-10, 12, 139
Submitting poems.... 141-143

**T**
Tools ....................19-22, 27, 29
Typefaces............................. 132

**U**
USA Today .....................30, 150

**V**
Viewpoint...................... 98-100
Vocabulary ................. 116-118

**W**
Website......................... 143-147
Wordstorming .. 18-19, 36-38